# Rebels with a Cause

# Ibérica

A. Robert Lauer
*General Editor*

Vol. 24

PETER LANG
New York • Washington, D.C./Baltimore • Boston
Bern • Frankfurt am Main • Berlin • Vienna • Paris

Bruce A. Boggs

# Rebels with a Cause

## Adam and Eve in Modern Spanish Literature

PETER LANG
New York • Washington, D.C./Baltimore • Boston
Bern • Frankfurt am Main • Berlin • Vienna • Paris

**Library of Congress Cataloging-in-Publication Data**

Boggs, Bruce A.
Rebels with a cause: Adam and Eve
in modern Spanish literature / Bruce A. Boggs.
p. cm. — (Ibérica; vol. 24)
Includes bibliographical references.
1. Spanish literature—Classical period, 1500-1700—History and criticism.
2. Spanish literature—18th century—History and criticism. 3. Spanish
literature—19th century—History and criticism. 4. Adam (Biblical figure)—
In literature. 5. Eve (Biblical figure)—In literature. 6. Myth in literature.
I. Title. II. Series: Ibérica (New York, N.Y.); vol. 24.
PQ6066.B63    860.9'352—dc21    96-53917
ISBN 0-8204-3484-1
ISSN 1056-5000


**Die Deutsche Bibliothek-CIP-Einheitsaufnahme**

Boggs, Bruce A.:
Rebels with a cause: Adam and Eve in modern Spanish literature /
Bruce A. Boggs. –New York; Washington, D.C. /Baltimore; Boston; Bern;
Frankfurt am Main; Berlin; Vienna; Paris: Lang.
(Ibérica; Vol. 24)
ISBN 0-8204-3484-1
NE: GT

The paper in this book meets the guidelines for permanence and durability
of the Committee on Production Guidelines for Book Longevity
of the Council of Library Resources.

Printed in the United States of America.

# Contents

# Preface

José de Espronceda's poetic masterwork of Spanish Romanticism, *El diablo mundo* (1840), introduces its central character, the old and disillusioned don Pablo, who in a strange vision is promised the gift of immortality. He awakes metamorphosed into a young, robust, and innocent stranger whom the poet calls Adán. Finding himself immediately at odds with society, the newly-minted man is cast into prison where he takes up company with criminals and rogues. So, in Espronceda's poem, the character Adán recalls the Biblical Adam, the first rebel and the primordial delinquent; however, in the process of his indoctrination into society, this Romantic Adán does not lose his noble innocence, for Espronceda created a unique character that combined both the innocent or pre-lapsarian notion of Adam and the criminal or post-lapsarian aspect, a character that defies death yet suffers the frustrations, emotions, and metaphysical anguish of mortal beings. This imaginative portrayal of the hero as sublime rebel is drawn according to the aesthetic ideals of the Liberal Romantics. Joaquín Casalduero in his *Forma y visión de* El diablo mundo *de Espronceda* has noted the affiliation between the romantics and the Adamic figure: Lord Byron, Espronceda, and their lot are drawn to the Biblical first man because they consider themselves culturally unadulterated, unfettered by the past and its trappings; they are "new" men in the sense that they feel free to explore the world from their own personal, creative perspectives. Espronceda's portrayal of Adán and Salada, the fallen woman, and their experiences in the corrupted world suggest a much more complex relationship between the nineteenth-century poem and the Biblical text from which Espronceda borrowed his notions of an innocent rebel. Here the Adamic myth merges with the Promethean myth and any notion of a "Fall" from grace becomes meaningless for the Promethean rebel brings into question the absolute goodness of God.

Some thirty-three years after Espronceda published *El diablo mundo*, *La caída de Adán*, an epic poem based on the Biblical story of the Fall of man, was published in Barcelona by Víctor Rosselló. In this more recent text, the poet depicts a more orthodox Adán in a poem in which religious sentiment and didactic intent are most evident since the reader is advised that the work is intended to serve the glory of God and the "provecho moral para los lectores" (Rosselló 5-6). Rosselló's poem, a literary recounting of the story of the first humans in the Garden of Eden, is more closely related to the ancient Celestial

Cycle where the Creation, the Rebellion of the Angels, and the Fall of Man were reproduced as actual events in the scheme of Christian history. To say that *El diablo mundo*, and *La caída de Adán*, are linked only by a common theme invites an inquiry into the more problematic question of what does the story of Adam and Eve really say. Whether the "literary" character is portrayed as a pre-lapsarian innocent man who is motivated by instinct, the post-lapsarian "sinner" in exile, or the first man as rebel bandit, the prototype of these Adamic characters, perceived in light of its manifestations in Western culture, is not as simplistic, especially in the Judeo-Christian exegetical traditions, as it appears in the Biblical narration.

The plight of Adam and Eve, the central figures of the creation tale, and the relationship between the first humans and subsequent generations has been a subject of interest for Spanish writers for centuries. "Adán celebra en el limbo la venida del mesías" and "Triste estaba el padre Adán", penned by Bartolomé Torres Naharro (1476?-1531?) in the sixteenth century, are but two examples of numerous short poems commenting on the supposed condition of Adam and Eve before, during, and after their transgression. Juan de Padilla (1468-1522?) wrote poetry about the first sin and its terrible consequences for humanity. In a much lighter vein Francisco de Quevedo cleverly seized upon Adam's unique "birth" as a pretext to extol the fortunes of the only married man in human history without a mother-in-law ("Padre Adán"), as well as to comment on the nature of modern love ("Adán en paraíso, vos en huerto").

In searching for insight into the themes, the messages, or the "aboutness" of the Genesis narrative or its figures, it must be remembered that all of our notions about Adam and Eve are the result of various traditions, each borrowing from and contributing to each other over a period of time. The Biblical creation tale itself pales in comparison to the more twenty centuries of interpretational writings that would seek to understand the first humans and their experiences in that fabled garden. "In the beginning": three simple words that sound out a familiar, formulaic invitation to a fantastic realm of pre-time and pre-place; a terse introduction to the strange narrative of the creation of the earth and its first inhabitants; the Biblical explanation of many pertinent questions, is a common place of western culture because it is a story that has fascinated and perplexed us for over three millennia. Perhaps no single narrative has come close to generating such a vast amount of interpretational writing and speculative energy as has this pithy tale of desire and authority, of loss and exile. But what is the history of this Judeo-Christian "beginning of history"? The structural elements of the Genesis are so familiar to us that we, like the Spaniards who re-created them in dramatic and poetic forms, mistakenly take them for granted. This odd narrative of Eve's desire to obtain knowledge, of God's fear and prohibition, of Adam's acquiescence, and of God's punitive wrath presents us with some seemingly profound mysteries.

The first chapter of this study traces the development of the figures of Adam and Eve from mythological characters in the Levantine oral tradition (before 950 BC) to their emergence as Christian symbols. This entails an examination of many of the narrative enigmas long associated with the Genesis text: the two acts of creation of humans known as Genesis A and B; the birth of Eve from Adam's side; the talking serpent and its relationship to the "Mother of all life"; the presence of two trees, only one of which is prohibited; and the whimsical God. Adam and Eve are shown to function in multiple roles, namely, as (1) central figures in a culturally significant myth that functioned as a part of a larger structural paradigm in artistic texts; (2) as theological signs charged with diverse symbolical values that often informed the artistic texts; and (3), as mytho-poetic symbols of primitivism, incorporating the myth of paradise that focuses attention on the relationship between humanity and the socio-cultural environment. Theoretical explanations of these narrative elements point out the importance of the iconotrophic process, the incorporation and the misreading of the symbols of one culture by another, and deliberate textual editing-out of elements that were found undesirable. The origins of the notions of evil, lost paradise, and Original Sin, all extraneous to the narrative, are results of the inconotropic manipulation of the Genesis narrative as well.

The textual explication of the Genesis A and B narratives owes much to the theories of myth criticism, such as those of Paul Ricoeur (*The Symbolism of Evil*), Northrop Frye (*The Great Code*), David Rosenberg and Harold Bloom (*The Book of J*), as well as the work of Joseph Campbell. Human cultures create and use stories for specific purposes; thus, there are no politically neutral narratives. Mythic narratives are functional elements of societies, whereby the relevance of a given narrative is not fixed, but rather will vary according to the cultural value that a society places on it at a given point in time. If it is true, as mythographers suggest, that each generation tends to read its own interpretation into a myth, then we can begin to explain the resilience and incredible staying-power of these puzzling creation stories. By studying the relationship of the Genesis creation myths to previous narratives in the Levantine oral tradition, the history and cultural vitality of the notions of evil, Original Sin, and the Fall, this study proposes to explicate the "message" of the Adamic dramatic and poetic re-creations of the story at a given point in time marked by the publication of the Spanish texts. I will concentrate particularly on structural aspects of the literary adaptations in order to show how the formal changes in these Adamic works are related to the "mythic" qualities of the tale. The functionality of the Adamic myth, its significance and importance to a particular society is viewed as a controlling element in the continuation or adaptation of the narrative. In addition, each work will be studied in light of the religious and aesthetic climates of each period in order to gauge the importance of the figures and the Genesis poetic myth within the period.

Since the object of this work is quite specific, it must necessarily encompass a broad historical perspective. This study examines Spanish versions of the Genesis creation story that occur principally in dramatic and poetic representations most often during a span of some three hundred years from approximately 1578 to 1873. This chronological period is not random; for while it would be nearly impossible to consider all the literary manifestations of this prevalent theme in the Castilian language, some genres, major works, and historical time frames stand out. The beginning of this period is marked by the date of compilation of the *Códice de Autos Viejos* (1578), which includes *autos* that utilize the Biblical narrative to dramatize tenets of Christian doctrine or, simply, to recreate in brief dramatic form the "history" of the first humans and their role in the Christian scheme of salvation. The proliferation of a western "culture of guilt" as proposed by Jean Delumeau in *Sin and Fear: the Emergence of Western Guilt Culture*, centers the Adam and Eve narrative as a foundational "historical" event, the knowledge of which can be used to modify the moral behavior of the general populace. Representational concerns such as characterization, description, and setting are subordinate to the concise portrayal of the Biblical message.

At the end of the period (1873) is *La caída de Adán*, by Víctor Rosselló, the text that represents the last literary adaptation of the myth of the Fall in the nineteenth-century Spain. Within the designated period of this study, some of Spain's major dramatists and poets have recreated the story of Adam and Eve, molding the language and structural elements of the ancient narrative into a more immediate and contemporary form, simultaneously altering the components of the Biblical tale as well as some of the extraneous notions associated with it. In all, the Biblical creation story became the paradigm for four *auto sacramentales*, two *comedias*, and at least five epic poems by some of the country's strongest writers. From its inception in the anonymous Spanish *auto*, the story of Adam and Eve was transformed by Lope de Vega and Vélez de Guevara into the three-act *comedia nueva*. Here, not only the aesthetics of the *comedia* but also the prolific mind of Lope are important considerations in his *La creación del mundo y primera culpa del hombre* (1618). Analysis of this work will show that the "historical" message-driven narrative takes on elements of biographical drama and the representation of Adam and Eve as individuals, undermines the myth's symbolical elements used to communicate its moral messages. A similar work written by Vélez de Guevara at about the same time (*La creación del mundo*) provides an example of an improvisational *comedia de repente*, a marked contrast and testament to Lope's original adaptation.

The belated discovery of *Paradise Lost* and its reception by the Spanish *Ilustrados* in the eighteenth century is the impetus for subsequent literary creations of the Fall story, as members of the Seville School stage a poetry contest in 1796 which has as its aim the creation of an epic poem about the theme of lost innocence to be composed in the style of Milton's masterpiece. Two of Spain's most distinguished poets of the *Academia de Letras Humanas de Sevilla*, Alberto Lista and Félix José Reinoso, submit separate poems both entitled *La inocencia perdida*. The winning poem by Reinoso has been called that writer's most important poetic accomplishment. An analysis of these poems will be treated along with the first attempts in Spain at translation of Milton's *Paradise Lost*, by Jovellanos, and that work's reception. While considerably inferior to Milton's talent, Reinoso's and Lista's texts attest to a shift in the cultural vitality of the Adamic myth as the function moves from moralistic to aesthetic concerns. Still in the tradition of the Celestial Cycle, the two versions of *La inocencia perdida* combine elements of the cosmic battle between God and Satan with the creation of the first humans, portraying God as the epic hero.

The treatment of Original Sin, evil, and lost paradise became important elements of these Spanish texts. However, when Spanish poets and dramatists re-wrote the poetic myth of Adam and Eve's transgression, they did so according to aesthetic precepts and taste dictated by genre and contemporary style. These literary re-countings of the Biblical tale, especially in dramatic form, had to overcome some major narrative obstacles that the Genesis presented, such as the representation of God, the talking snake and its association with Satan, the creation of the humans and the representation of angels. Inevitably individual talent and creativity were a critical ingredient in each of the adaptations in order to fill in the narrative spaces or gaps in the Biblical narrative, and inevitably, as with the case of Milton, the literary adaptations altered or even distorted the orthodox message that the text was intended to convey. Espronceda's unique depiction of Adam and Eve and the Adamic myth is an example of conscious manipulation or distortion of the messages of the Genesis creation narratives. While this poem does not follow closely the narrative paradigm of the Genesis narration as do other literary texts examined in this study, it does call attention to the Biblical Adam as its protagonist, and takes as its subject, the human condition, combining elements of the Creation myth, the myth of the Fall of the Rebel Angels, and the myth of the Fall of Man into a poem that has been interpreted as anti-Christian. A pupil of Lista, Espronceda probably read *La inocencia perdida* and Milton's *Paradise Lost*. To date, only one critic, Francisco García Lorca, has studied the relationship of *El diablo mundo* to the Adam and Eve narrative, identifying what he calls "paradise themes". In light of García Lorca's findings, the present study demonstrates that Espronceda's poem is a unique manifestation of the larger Adamic tradition in Spain. As an allegorization of the human experience, incorporating within itself a pagan creation of man by a feminine earth-goddess, and an inverse sense of culpability where Man and Woman blame and condemn God for creating evil and death, *El diablo mundo* is a decidedly Romantic reaction to previous Adamic texts.

Finally, with its insistence on the corruption of man, Víctor Rosselló follows a lengthy European tradition of portraying a theologically derived Adam and Eve as an expression of the culture of fear and sin where the human condition in the world is scorned because of fear of the Hell of a wrathful and judgmental God. Both Romantic and anti-Romantic, Rossello's *La caída de Adán* may be read as a reaction to Espronceda's poem and to progressive ideas regarding religion in general. By recasting its characters and events in historical, biographical, and spiritual language, this adaptation seeks to reinvest the Adamic myth with renewed cultural significance, proving the loss of the vitality and cultural relevance for the enlightened part of Spanish society at this time.

# Chapter One:

## From Mythological Character
## To Biblical Symbol

The profusion of references and allusions to the mythical figures of Adam and Eve in western art and literature is remarkable; however, it is almost certain that these figures would not be recognizable to a large part of the western world if they were somehow excised from the Genesis creation narrative and its etiological function of grounding and conveying principle moral values of the Jewish and Christian religions. Adam and Eve may not be viewed as mere mythological characters belonging to a simple yet puzzling narrative, for they are also powerful cultural symbols inextricably linked to the Genesis narrative and also to an associated corpus of conceptual sub-texts which derive from the speculative writings of the Biblical exegetical tradition. Dürer entitled his engraving of Adam and Eve "Original Sin," and most painters depicted the first couple in their edenic paradise, often freezing the action of the narrative at the crucial moment before Adam plunged Humanity into the Fall from God's grace. While the Fall, earthly paradise, and Original Sin have come to be synonymous with the figures of Adam and Eve; surprisingly, these concepts are all extraneous to the narrative as it occurs in the Book of Genesis. Yet they remain an integral part of the "narrative" for most readers for whenever Adam and Eve are represented in any artistic form, they are always accompanied by these exegetical sub-texts or motifs lurking within our cultural frame of reference.

These sub-texts are the symbolic values to which the Genesis narrative has been reduced, its symbolical meaning. The figures of Adam and Eve never stand alone without these symbolic values leading us back to the Genesis narrative. Indeed, the myth, its principal actors, and the symbols are, for all practical purposes, indivisible entities, comprising a part of the greater conceptual web that makes up the intellectual fare of all Christian societies. In the Christian history of salvation, the story of Adam and Eve became the etiological myth to explain the beginning of evil, the element that separated humanity from its perfect God and thus necessitated the coming of the Savior. Why was the story of Adam associated with the separation of humanity from God by early Jews and Christians? And why did the notions of evil and Original Sin become equivalent to the figures of Adam and Eve? Where did the story originate? And how do we explain the unusual cast of characters and incidents in it? While a history of the exegesis of the tale of Adam and Eve and the concepts associated with it would be a task of seemingly heroic proportions, it is necessary and possible to understand, if only summarily, some of the questions surrounding the figure, the text, and its principal substructural motifs of evil and Original Sin.

In the earliest writings, the figure of Adam was not generally depicted as the historical first man, but rather as the genus, the neutral and nameless prototype. In the Torah, we are told that Yahweh formed the man (*ha-'adam*), from the soil (*ha-'adamah*); however, the etymology of the word "adam" remains uncertain. The root of the Hebrew word *'dm* expresses the color "red." That *ha-'adam* was said to have been formed from *ha-'adamah* might suggest the color of soil from which the "earthling" was formed. In Akkadian, *adamu* means "blood" and, according to the *Encyclopaedia Judaica*, may have a figurative meaning of "important, a noble person;" while in Old South Arabic the root *'dm* means "serf." Old Akkadian and Old Babylonian show occurrences of the personal names *A-da-mu*, *A-Dam-u*, and *'A-da-mu* (235). The Tanakh, or Hebrew Bible, was ambiguous in its usage of the common noun and the proper noun. The former was used generally while the latter occurred only in the genealogy of Chronicles (1:1). The Vulgate followed suit, according to Anthony D. York, generally translating 'adam' into 'man' with the exception of Joshua and Zechariah (104). In the third century BCE the Septuagint, the oldest Greek version of the Old Testament, changed the common noun in Genesis 2:16 to the proper noun and the Vulgate then introduced 'Adam' in Genesis 2:19 (York 103). Although these nomenclatural changes occurred in the copying and translating of the early written texts of the Torah and the Bible, the characters within the creation story had already been shaped by the text itself. Harold Bloom has emphasized that despite the detrimental effects of repeated translation, Yahweh in the oldest written account of Adam and Eve is a literary character, drawn with the skill of a sophisticated narrator (Rosenberg and Bloom 12-14). Bloom's assumption of an individual author of the Adam and Eve story leads us from the sacrosanct realm of Holy Scripture to the more manageable terrain of imaginative literature with its sub-class of myth. It is within the structure of the study of myth that this simple yet enigmatic text may best be explained.

It is useful to perceive Eve and Adam first and foremost as characters of an ancient narrative which fulfills many of the definitive qualities of myth. William G. Doty defines myth as a "culturally important imaginal stor[y], conveying by means of metaphoric and symbolic diction, graphic imagery, and emotional conviction and participation, the primal, foundational accounts of aspects of the real, experienced world and humankind's roles and relative statuses within it"

(11). The importance placed upon certain myths by a society, or the value given to a particular myth, says Doty, is proportionate to the "sense of 'history'" communicated by it. This definition of history does not refer to "history as chronicle" but rather to "meaningful history." A myth endures in the minds of a people because the information that it conveys has been chosen, consciously or not, as the "most important symbolic interpretations, its quintessential codings of what 'means' the most to humankind out of the myriad of possibilities" (17). In addition, moral values often make up the information conveyed by myth—systems of belief are validated and protected especially by distancing them in time and space—by "referring them to a prototypical time of origins" and by "grounding them in a primordial scene that is not open to questioning" (Doty 30). When one looks closely at the myth of Adam and Eve presented in the Book of Genesis, it becomes obvious that its cosmogonic function is less important than its attempt to sanction a chosen pattern of belief. The creation of the world was already recounted in the first chapter of Genesis, so the second chapter could be given to the expression of other bits of history. The function of the 'meaning' in the story is essential to the understanding of it as myth. If a myth loses its symbolical value in a given society, then it no longer serves the purposes of the society that had sanctioned it. The myth of Adam and Eve became a part of the Judeo—Christian sacred writings—the Torah (also known as the Pentateuch) and the Old Testament (the Covenant)—because certain essential messages could be extrapolated from its narrative.

Placed within the context of mythological discourse, the story of Adam and Eve may be defined as a metaphorical narrative into whose concrete imagery was read an expression of the primal beginning of a real or imagined sense of innate and inherent human evil. The Israelites' experiences of evil vested the myth and its central figures with symbolic meaning. The narrative became culturally valued and was further sanctified by the 'emotional' investment and the acute 'participation' of the Rabbis and Christian leaders whose exegetical writings supplied myriad speculative possibilities to explain the myth's many enigmas. The subsequent ideas of evil and Original Sin emerged especially in the emotionally charged Christian writings after Christian leaders appropriated the Covenant and renamed it the Old Testament. While it is impossible to know the exact origin of an ancient myth and its meaning to early peoples, there is much information that has been discovered concerning the early written version of the tale of Adam and Eve and there is evidence that similar narratives may have circulated in the oral traditions of the Levant. A comparison between the two creation stories in Genesis will help to establish many of the central historical concepts that have been discovered regarding the myth.

The Christian notion of the creation as it is presented in the Book of Genesis presents a confusing array of incidents and personages that are best explained by the fact that Genesis recounts two distinct cosmogonies, two irreconcilable narratives that were undoubtedly the work of separate authors at separate times. The first chapter of the book, Genesis A, is concerned with the creation of the cosmos by God in six days beginning with nothing. In the formation of the Earth the element of chaos is introduced: the murky and watery "darkness [. . .] upon the face of the deep"[1] which God puts into order by the generation of light, the creation of the firmament, the plants, the celestial bodies, the animals, and finally, culminating in the simultaneous creation of woman and man. In contrast, the second narrative, Genesis B which begins with chapter 2:4, gives chronological precedence to the formation of the first man, the birds, and the animals before the event of the anomalous, surgical birth of the first woman from man's side as he lay anesthetized by the god.

Principally sky oriented, Genesis A portrays a transcendental supreme being known only as 'God,' who carries out the creation of the world with all of its many elements by the action of summoning, of speaking it into existence: a creation by the abstract logic of the spoken word by an ethereal supreme being that is manifested only in this conceptual, spoken environment. Genesis B, with its focus on earthly matters, requires an anthropomorphized god. Yahweh, the Hebrew name for God, is a direct descendant of the demigods—he interacts with the first humans, speaking directly to them, strolling through the garden in search of them; and, by necessity, this is a god who works with his hands, the laborer or artisan god, since he has formed man from the moist red clay of the earth. Yahweh and his earthy creation provide a pronounced contrast to the abstract God of the spoken word who creates by speech act. That the supposedly singular creation was manifested in the Covenant in two stories was surely disconcerting to early theologians, but the differences were explained away with creative speculation.

In the second story, the narrative elements in and of themselves are uncanny and puzzling. Paul Ricoeur in *The Symbolism of Evil* has labeled the Adamic narrative a "drama [with a] turbid ambiguity" (243), and Morris Freilich finds the characters and the events of the narrative illogical and incoherent, "bits of non-sense information" where a tempting and lying God goes into a "tantrum" when his creatures disobey him; a snake with the power of speech must struggle to convince a woman to go against God's mandate while a passive

Adam "grabs the fruit almost without a second thought." At once God is threat-ening and then apologetic, giving the people unneeded clothing and then throwing them out of the garden in order "to keep them away from a tree whose fruits have not previously been forbidden" (207-26). Freilich's ideas, a modern reader's critical perception of the story, emphasize the strange combination of characters and events that has intrigued and confounded ancient and modern people alike, and, in turn, has given rise to innumerable Rabbinical commentar-ies, Christian interpretations, homiletical writings and artistic manifestations. Because of its ambiguity and the importance placed upon it as a primal justifi-cation of evil, the story of the first people was subjected to intense scrutiny, both within and without the Church; writes J. M. Evans in Paradise Lost *and the Genesis Tradition*, and in the process, it "expanded in every conceivable direc-tion, undergoing almost as many transformations as it had interpreters" (10). Nevertheless, almost all speculation continued to revolve around the main themes of the Fall: Man's first transgression against God, lost Paradise, and the beginning of evil in an otherwise perfect creation by a singular God. The per-sistent ambiguities of the ancient text generated intense scrutiny through the centuries of the Christian era, as theologians attempted to understand the nature of the symbolical code that would help them to understand their universe.

## The Jahwist Text and the Remnants of Lost Traditions

While there is no agreement as to the date of the source of the Adam and Eve narrative, the earliest written text is found in the first book of the Hebrew Pentateuch that became the Book of Genesis. By contrasting the two creation stories, scholars have been able to determine a relative chronology of the texts. Not unlike the Old Testament, the Book of Genesis is a composite which is considered by some scholars to have been written over a period of about four hundred years, from the tenth century BCE to the fifth, during which time it was influenced by three principle authorial traditions. It is also held that the sources of this first book of the Old Testament belong to a more ancient tradition in which material was reinterpreted and incorporated into the Hebrew narrative (Lerner 162). The document thought to be the oldest part of the Pentateuch is the Jahwist text, so named for its labeling of the deity as Jahweh and for its Ju-dean origin. The Jahwist text, known to contemporary Biblical scholars as J, is a previously lost version of the Hebrew Bible consisting of Genesis, Exodus, and Numbers. The second source chronologically is the Elohist tradition, known as

E for its designation of the deity as *Elohim* ("the plural name used for Yah-weh") and because it is believed to represent the Ephraimite tradition. The E tradition, according to Rosenberg and Bloom, is responsible for the revision and censoring of J which brought the ancient text more in line with Hebrew mono-theism, while incorporating extraneous material (22). Lastly, there is the Priestly tradition, or P, which reinterpreted and combined the J and E narratives. The Priestly tradition is not considered by scholars to be an individual but rather a "school of priestly redactors in Jerusalem who may have worked for hundreds of years and completed the work in the seventh century BCE" (Lerner 162). Each tradition drew material from legend and folklore of the Levant cultures, whose written and oral traditions were extensive. Sometime around 450 BCE, the Pentateuch was created by the fusion of the various elements of the J, E, and P traditions (Lerner 162). If we classify the first five verses of Genesis by authorial tradition, we find that verses 2.4b through 2.25 and three, four, and 5.29 make up the J tradition. The E tradition modified the J material. The P authors were responsible for chapter one, verse one through chapter two, verse four; and chapter five, verse one to chapter five, verse twenty-eight. The contri-bution of the P tradition (fifth century BCE) is the creation of Genesis A and its conflation with the older B narrative to produce the two distinct cosmogonies of the Book of Genesis.

Of the three authorial traditions of the Old Testament, it is the Jahwist text that has most allured contemporary Biblical scholars with its original tone, its anthropomorphic gods and its unusual ironic flare. The Jahwist version is the oldest, more interesting of the Biblical cosmogonies and is believed to have been completed by 915 BCE. By circa 850 BCE, the theoretical beginning of the Elohist period, the imaginative narrative of the Jahwist tradition had been trans-formed. Both the Elohist and the Priestly traditions censored the politically un-desirable elements from J and coupled the narrative with a mixture of written sources that later became lost (Rosenberg and Bloom 22).

Taken in its entirety, the Jahwist text is considered by Biblical critics to be the literary jewel of the Bible, for they ascribe to it a style that could only be-long to a true literary artist. E. A. Speiser writes that the Jahwist text not only possesses much of the narrative content which has inspired the almost universal appeal of the Old Testament in the western world, but demonstrates a singular style as well (*Genesis* xxiv). The Jahwist narration of the first man and woman is, in the words of Evans, a "model of economy" where the dialogue gives the characters vividness while propelling the narration forward with each sentence. Only the essential elements are highlighted; nevertheless, one gets the feeling that there is some "underlying complexity" in the narration (13). Speiser classifies the Jahwist's style as "incisive [with the] economy and boldness of presentation" of an artist (xxvii). In *The Book of J*, Rosenberg and Bloom theorize that the Jahwist was a female poet, probably one of many at the employ of the Solomonic monarchy. Both purport that the Jahwist lived around the time of the court of Solomon's son and successor, King Rehoboam of Judah, and that her "astonishingly" distinct representation of women as well as her subtle irony suggest that she was not a professional scribe, but, most likely, a "sophisticated, highly placed member of the Solomonic elite" (9-48). The Jahwist's skill at narrative places her beyond the category of mere storyteller, for she distinguishes herself as a "creator of personalities (human and divine)" as well as a "national historian" who translates myth into history (Rosenberg and Bloom 13-14). The humor, based principally on irony and puns,[2] gives the Jahwist narrative a sophistication that is lacking in the Priestly authors' mundane chronicle of the creation with its "stereo-typed formulae and monotonous redundancies" (Evans 14). The theory of the Jahwist as a single author remains purely hypothetical. However, the theory of three authorial traditions does lead directly to the question of the conscious manipulation of the narrations—a hypothesis which helps explain the many ambiguities found in the text.

Given the fantastic elements of the story, the talking snake, the strolling Yahweh, and the anomalous birth of Eve, it is not so unusual that the Jahwist's protagonists do not die from their transgression as Yahweh had predicted; rather they become aware of their nakedness somehow suggesting that sexuality is the first newly acquired "evil" thing of which the humans become knowledgeable. Interestingly, it is the "subtle" serpent who is most forthcoming with the way to acquire the strange wisdom that suddenly makes them naked, and it is this new knowledge and the means of acquiring it which somehow cause the first couple to be exiled from the bountiful garden of paradise. What are the antecedents from which the Jahwist could have borrowed these unusual elements and incidents which came to make up the second Biblical creation story, and which formed the literary basis for the tradition of the Fall of man?

In the Jahwist narrative we are given only a fragmented view of the lives of the first humans. There is evidence attesting to the existence of a written Adamic tradition in the ancient Levant preceding the earliest known cuneiform text, and it is probable that the myth of Adam and Eve circulated in some form in the oral traditions of the Levant cultures long before it was written down by any Hebrew author sometime around 915 BCE. What is the nature of the traditional material from which the authorial sources borrowed in their emendation of the text? If the existence of the legendary first humans was believed as historical fact by the ancient people of the Levant, then it is logical to assume that this belief would have engendered stories that sought to fill in the details as to the circumstances of the first humans' lives in exile. In fact it was believed that Adam and Eve lived long lives outside the forbidden garden, according to evidence attributed to some non-extant texts that dealt with the legendary figures in their garden paradise. The lost Scroll of Paradise (*Sefer Gan Eden*), which predates the Jahwist text by some one hundred and fifty years, supposedly gave accounts of the primordial couple dealing with two separate talking snakes. In *The Lost Book of Paradise: Adam and Eve in the Garden of Eden*, David Rosenberg studies the evidence of the existence of this text finding in it the "original" of the Biblical Eden story. Believed extant for several hundred years, the Scroll of Paradise was the subject of commentary by a Hebraic midrash and aggadah which, in turn, mention another scroll, the Scroll of the History of Adam, which recounted Adam and Eve's experiences outside of Eden (127). Rosenberg adds that while almost all traces of these early texts have disappeared from the Bible, Biblical commentaries dating to the Kabbalah of the Middle Ages evince the texts' existence and that ninth-century portions of the *Midrash Shir ha-Shirim* (Commentary on the Song of Solomon) "names the two shameless and equal lovers in Solomon's Biblical poem as Adam and Eve, suggesting that the Song of Solomon was modeled upon the Book of Paradise" (xi).

The distinguished anthropologist Sir George Frazer has also linked the tale of the first humans to more ancient narratives belonging to the folklore traditions of the Levant cultures. This expert mythologist offers what seems to be a credible explanation for the two trees, the serpent, and the relationship between these elements and the humans, with his theory that the story is an amalgamation of two separate narratives. In his comparison of the Adam and Eve story with other narratives from the folklore tradition of the Levant, Frazer proposes that the trees hold the key to understanding the narrative: Eden contains not one but two forbidden trees, the first is the tree of knowledge of good and evil, forming the center around which the main conflict of the drama takes place. But the Jahwist author does not seem to know nor does s/he hint at any reasons for the prohibition against eating from this tree. The prohibition is simply a given, as are the talking reptile and the strolling Yahweh. In the background of this narrative—and presented almost as an afterthought—is the second tree, the tree of immortality, which according to Frazer, seems to have been "clipped . . . almost past recognition" out of the existing tale when the two separate narrations were combined into one (47). Frazer concurs with most contemporary critics regarding the story's primary function as an etiological myth explaining the beginning of death. His theory, however, links the tale with one from an older Semite narrative in which the magic plant forbidden to the first humans was the tree of mortality and not the tree of knowledge of good and evil. Hence God's warning that anyone who eats its fruit will die. In the first story, says Frazer, humankind was encouraged to eat from all trees of the garden, including the tree of immortality (the tree of Life so jealously protected by Yahweh), so that humans might live forever like the gods. This would have been the case except for the serpent who, according to Frazer, had a stake in deceiving man. The Creator wanted the humans to have the choice between mortality or immortality, but in order to help them choose the right tree, he commanded the snake to carry a message to humans, telling them specifically not to eat from the tree of mortality ("eat from it . . . and on that day death touches you").[3] But the sagacious reptile changed the message telling the humans that they would not die. When the humans ate the fruit of death, the tree of immortality was left for the reptile, who ate and now sheds its skin as a renewal of youth that grants it the gift of everlasting life.

The story in this form still respects the motif of free will that is found in the Jahwist's version. It burdens humankind with the freedom of choice between immortality and mortality. However, the two trees and the incomprehensible prohibition regarding the first tree (the tree that the Jahwist changed to the tree of knowledge of good and evil) now are consistent and logical. The motif of a serpent that achieves immortality by deception is also found in a more ancient story, the "literary monument" of the Semites—the Gilgamesh epic. In this tale, Gilgamesh was told of a plant of immortality which he planned to acquire for himself, but before he could do so, a serpent stole the plant. Frazer provides further evidence from folklore in his comparison of the tale with structural forms which he labels "the Story of the Perverted Message" and the "Story of the Cast Skin," also etiological myths about the beginning of death (46-52).

One of the most notable characteristics of the Jahwist cosmogony is the innocent, almost impish tone that brings to mind the genres of the fairy tale and the fable. The fable normally features non-human beings as its characters, and a prime ingredient of the fairy tale is magic and deception (Cuddon 256-58). Yahweh and the serpent could well be folkloristic precursors of the non-human personages of Greek fable, for they are presented as literary characters, personified to function as credible elements in a story with a moralistic twist. Yahweh shares more qualities with the humans than with the gods, and it is easy to understand why the Elohist redactors would want to censure the Jahwist's deity, substituting the distant, transcendent *Elohim* (which has been translated as the "Lord God"), in place of the fearful and jealous Yahweh whose lack of omniscience and omnipotence are blatant. Another element related to the fairy tale is the admonition/ transgression motif, which, according to Joseph Campbell, is a structural motif found in fairy tales throughout the world (110). The characters exhibit a childlike naiveté befitting newly created beings, and Yahweh is both paternal and immature. When Adam and Eve are given the warning, it is presumed that they will not heed it, therefore leading to the aphorism or the moral conclusion that is a feature of this genre.

Still other scholars have found interesting analogues to the Jahwist cosmology in the mythology of the ancient peoples of the Levant. A closer look at the symbols of the trees, the serpent, and their association with the cults of the Great Goddess, suggests that the text is, in the words of Merlin Stone, "most certainly a tale with a point of view, and with a most biased proclamation for its ending" (198). What many scholars find in the Book of Genesis generally, and in the creation stories in particular, is evidence of a cover-up: an attempt by Hebrew editors to manipulate an existent system of symbols, to sublimate and purge from local myths certain aspects which were contrary to the nature of their own beliefs. The gaps or anomalies in the story, according to Robert Graves in his *Adam's Rib and Other Anomalous Elements in the Hebrew Creation Myth*, all "suggest that the author of these chapters was faced with the difficult task of welding together various unrelated traditions into a new official cosmogony" (1). It is probable that instead of creating new myths, existing tales were appropriated and the material was altered. Narrative elements were manipulated so that the symbolic message might correspond to the belief system of the dominating culture.

What was the nature of these symbols and mythologies? John A. Phillips has noted that the struggle for power between masculine and feminine deities is a common theme in the creation myths of the ancient Near Eastern cultures, with the masculine gods usually defeating the feminine deities (4). One of the most famous examples of this paradigm is a myth that influenced the narrative of Genesis A, and which is considered to be the source of the imagery of chaos and the unformed, watery "darkness" at the beginning of the story of the P cosmogony. Phillips sums up the details of the myth that is known as the *Enûma elish*:

> . . . the Mesopotamian saga of creation, the *Enûma elish*, narrates the destruction of the terrible Tiamat, the dragon-mother of all creation, in

the cataclysmic struggle with Marduk, the young warrior-god who has taken for himself the potency and fealty of the other deities. When at last he has defeated the treacherous Tiamat, he creates the world by splitting her carcass into earth and sky; she herself becomes the primordial matter of the universe. (5)

This Sumero-Akkadian theogony is a "type" of myth that Ricoeur has described as the victory of "order over chaos," which is an adequate description of the creation of the world in the Priestly text or Genesis A (176). The *Biblia castellana* of 1420 demonstrates the tenor of that ancient passage: "En el principio crió el Señor los cielos et la tierra, et la tierra era vana et vazía, et tenebra sobre faces del abismo. Et el Spiritu del Señor era rretraido sobre faces de las aguas."[4]    Other creation myths of this type from Mesopotamia portray the creation of the human world as a derivative of the primal theogonies, where out of the gods' battles for power, the human realm is magically given being. The beginning of matter and life in the priestly redacted Genesis A is different, however, for the Hebrew monotheists could not permit their Lord God of Genesis to struggle with other forces, because he must be an omnipotent, perfect, and supreme deity. Thus, in place of the internal struggles for power and the theocide that result in the creation, the Jewish and Christian theologies strayed and advocated the *creatio ex nihilo* by their solitary God. (Phillips 5-6). The imagery of chaos and darkness found in Genesis A is almost all that remains of the struggle for powers between the former gods of the Sumerian pantheon. The story of the first humans and Yahweh (Genesis B), however, was not completely purged of its polytheist elements.

The Old Testament is scattered with remnants of the mythologies of Mesopotamia: truncated shards which attest to a power struggle, out of which Yahweh, the Tiamat-like warrior-god must rise above the dominant Mother Goddess of the Levant. "No one familiar with the mythologies of the goddess of the primitive, ancient, and Oriental worlds," says Campbell, "can turn to the Bible without recognizing counterparts on every page, transformed, however, to render an argument contrary to the older faiths" (9). In *Adam's Rib and Other Anomalous Elements in the Hebrew Creation Myth*, Graves has noted that Genesis "still harbors vestigial accounts of ancient gods and goddesses—disguised as men, women, angels, monsters, or demons (12). He goes on to explain some of the historical aspects of the "patriarchal ancestors" who first dealt with the religions of the goddesses and the remnants of Levant mythology still present in the Jewish religion. We must consider, says Graves, that masculine monotheism required the Jews to "recast all the popular myths concerned with the cult of the immortal, variously-named Canaanite Love-goddess" know as Ishtar, Isis, Aphrodite and other names, and this operation proved to be a formidable job.

There are interesting links between the most important elements of the Biblical tale of Eden and the worship of the "Great Goddess," or the "Divine Ancestress," revered from Neolithic times (7000 BCE) until around 500 AD. The trees in Eden have analogues in the religions that worshipped the Goddess. The symbol of the tree was present in the Neolithic and High Bronze Age cultures and was read cosmologically and mystically as the world axis, the converging point of all opposites. In other accounts, the tree represents, or is interpreted as conveying, other forms of knowledge (Campbell 105). The Genesis tree of opposites is the source of knowledge of good and evil, and Frazer's suggestion that the trees represented both mortality and immortality also falls in line with this belief. Campbell's descriptions of some iconic seals found in the Near East point to similarities among the icons of the tree, the serpent, the woman and the Jahwist narrative. One seal shows a garden in which female divinities pluck fruit from a tree and present the fruit to a woman. A Sumerian seal shows a "Bronze Age view of the garden of innocence" in which two fruits, the fruit of enlightenment and the fruit of immortal life are suspended from a central tree. On each side of the tree are deities, one of which is the female Gula-Bau, who sits before a snake; the male is her son-husband who is "Lord of the tree of life, the everdying, ever-resurrected Sumerian god who is the archetype of incarnate being" (Campbell 13-14).

The serpent that became the temptress of Eve, besides having an analogue in the serpent-thief of the magic plant in Gilgamesh, is a principle ingredient in some of the cults of the fertility Goddess, and may also be linked to the evil serpents of Semitic demonology; however, there is a consensus, remarks Evans, that the Jahwist was not thinking of the later association of the serpent with Satan (19). The reptile was deified in the Levant some seven thousand years before the composition of the Book of Genesis, according to Stone. There were serpent goddesses: Nina, or Inanna, in ancient Sumeria and the Babylonian-Kassite mythology described Tiamat, the first divine being, as a serpent or dragon. "The use of the cobra in the religion of the Goddess in Egypt was so ancient that the sign that preceded the name of any Goddess was the cobra (i.e. a picture of a cobra was the hieroglyphic sign for the word Goddess)" (Stone 201). This animal which is often depicted as somehow more "subtle" than the other creatures, is commonly associated with the phallus; however, Stone notes that it was more often linked to "wisdom and prophetic counsel rather than fertility and growth" and was the representation of the goddess Nidaba, the scribe of the Sumerian heaven (199). And in Greece at the Delphi, the "woman who brought forth the oracles of divine wisdom was called the Phthia. Coiled about the tripod stool upon which she sat was the snake known as Python" (Stone 199-203). The association of the serpent with the deity and prophetic revelation was substantive. Both Hebrew and Arabic have terms for magic which are derived from the words meaning serpent (Stone 212). The Goddess, the Great Procreatress, the Giver of Life, had long been in association with the serpent, itself an immortal god of reproduction, a divine counselor of the Goddess, a symbol of the mystery of that other-worldly force from which springs life.

For Stone, Campbell, and Phillips, the role portrayed by Eve in the story, her relationship to the tree and the serpent, is the key to understanding the puzzling incidents of the narrative and the importance of the tale to the newer Hebrew and Christian monotheistic cults. Eve is generally considered by these scholars to be an anthropomorphism of the earth goddess, deified by early agricultural societies that associated the seemingly autonomous reproduction of human life by woman with the fecundity of the earth. For Phillips, the story of Genesis B is principally the story of Eve, who as the most important character in the conflict, is the "heart" of the concept of Woman in the western world (xiii). Her beginnings are not to be found in Adam's rib but rather in Adam's declaration that she be called the "Mother of All the Living," an alias by which the primal goddess was known. The association of Eve to the Earth Goddess may explain in part the misogynist qualities found in the Genesis story. The Jahwist does not hide his/her "contempt" for woman, remarks Frazer. "The lateness of her creation, and the irregular and undignified manner of it-made out of a piece of her lord and master, after all the lower animals had been created in a regular and decent manner" is proof that the writer was biased; and when s/he subsequently attributes "all the misfortunes and sorrows of the human race to the credulous folly and unbridled appetite of its first mother," then, says Frazer, the Jahwist's misogyny has proved to be even more severe (5).

According to Robert Graves and Raphael Patai who study the myth in their *Hebrew Myths: The Book of Genesis*, both the Greek and the Hebrew cultures share a common theme of the "gradual reduction of women from sacred beings to chattels." Pandora (All Gifts)—also a name for the "Creatrix"—was slandered with the crime of unleashing disasters and woes on the world. Likewise, Eve is humiliated for causing man to transgress against his God. In order to further "disguise" Eve's sanctity, Graves and Patai add, the Genesis redactors presented her as molded from man's rib, which is an "anecdote based appar-

ently on the word *tsela*, meaning both 'rib' and 'a stumbling.' Still later mythographers insisted that she was formed from Adam's barbed tail" (15).

For Campbell, the role of Eve as temptress and subordinate in the myth is
one example among many demonstrating that the patriarchal Hebrew culture
sought to legitimize its belief in one god by denigrating the symbols normally
held in opposition to the monotheist cults. Eve is the "missing anthropomorphic
aspect" of the Goddess; consequently Adam had to be both her son and her
spouse, because the legend of the rib, he writes, is a definite "patriarchal inver-
sion of the myth of the hero born from the Goddess Earth, who returns to her to
be reborn" (30). The first woman is implicated in the downfall of man and must
be officially ostracized, relegated to an inferior status in the hierarchy; the serpent, a former deity, must be condemned as the lowest and most despicable of
creatures. The birth process is inverted, transferred to man, placing the female as
third in line from her two "creators": the solitary Yahweh, and the life-giving
Adam. Stone concludes her study stating that the forbidden knowledge that the
first couple gained was indeed sexual, basing her evidence on the role of Eve as
the lost "Mother of All Living":

> So into the myth of how the world began, the story that the Levites of-
> fered as the explanation of the creation of all existence, they place the
> advisory serpent and the woman who accepted its counsel, eating of the
> tree that gave her the understanding of what 'only the gods knew'—the
> secret of sex—*how* to create life. (217)

Also, in the story of Adam and Eve, this vivid, concise, and ancient narrative
with its seemingly distinct elements, Campbell finds what he designates as the
first characteristic feature of Occidental mythology, whether it be Greco-Roman
or Judean:

> In the West, [. . .] the principle of indeterminacy represented by the
> freely willing, historically effective hero not only gained but held the
> field, and has retained it to the present. . . . This victory of the principle
> of free will, together with its moral corollary of individual responsibil-
> ity, establishes the first distinguishing characteristic of specifically Oc-
> cidental myth [including Greek, Roman, Celtic, Germanic, and the Se-
> mitic peoples of the Levant]. For whether we think of the victories of
> Zeus and Apollo, Theseus, Perseus, Jason, and the rest, over the drag-
> ons of the Golden Age, or turn to that of Yahweh over Leviathan, the

lesson is equally of a self-moving power greater than the force of any earthbound serpent destiny. All stand [in opposition to] the daimones of the fertility of Earth. (24)

So in the great heroes' triumph over the dragons or in the victory of Yahweh over the Leviathan serpent, we find the same paradigm of the triumph of Good over the forces of the Earth, accompanied by an abhorrence toward the worship of the Earth, with all its implied darkness, disease, death, and its impenetrable mysteries of procreation (Campbell 24-25).

Thus, the priestly writers of Genesis did not consciously invent the unusual elements of the texts; rather, they borrowed existing material from earlier cults, including the creation myths, and adapted and edited them to suit their own religious and moral agendas. The transcendental God of the Hebrew religion was promoted as the only god and the power struggle between the forces of light over dark, between good and evil were consciously hidden in the newly emerging cult of Yahweh. We may conclude then that the Genesis cosmogonies as well as other Old Testament myths show evidence that the narratives themselves may have resulted in part from the process of iconotropy—the misinterpretation of icons and emblems, or the incorporation of and the misreading of the symbols of one culture by another. As Robert Graves explains, the Book of Genesis can only be understood if we take into account that its sacred symbols and ancient icons have suffered repeated misreadings at the hands of Ecclesiastic authorities who would seek to interpret the ancient myths according to their own political and religious agendas (*Adam's Rib* 1). How much of the narrative may be owed to earlier traditions and what were the precursor myths are unknown. In dealing with this myth, the Rabbis are first concerned with the same questions as the contemporary readers, notes Evans: "who or what is the serpent, and how do the trees of knowledge and life relate to the rest of the story?" However, their ultimate interest was found not in the text's meaning, rather in the "reinterpretation of [its] symbols" (21).

The analogies between Eve and the Earth-goddess, the serpent and the association of the female deities with the two trees—the tree of opposites and the tree of life—all seem to lead logically to the conclusion that the manipulation of one or more existing narratives may have resulted in the uncanny combination of characters and incidents which make up the Adam and Eve story. Whether the iconotrophic process is conscious or not is impossible to tell. In making the case for her hypothesis that the Hebrew story fulfills a political intent to suppress matriarchy, women, and the goddess religions which had been prevalent in many cultures from prehistoric times to early historic times, Stone remarks on the original intent of the myth: "[it] had actually been designed to be used in the continuous Levite battle to suppress the female religion," adding that it is "a more updated version of the dragon or serpent myth whose vestiges are found in the Biblical Psalms and the book of Job" (198). The ambiguity in the myth was an advantage from the point of view of the Rabbis, says Evans, "allowing them to read into it whatever doctrinal significance they wished to find there" (21). The patriarchal Hebrew culture seeks to legitimize its belief in one god by placing the god in opposition to the many goddess cults that it abhors; thus woman must be associated with deception, the deep, dark, unknown chaos of the Other, and must be 'officially' and sanctifiably ostracized and relegated to an inferior status in the chain of being. Whether the process was a conscious manipulation of older symbols, or whether it was a unconscious union of pieces of narratives in order to reinterpret their beliefs, we cannot know. From its ancient first text, and its associated symbols of the goddess cults, the cult of Yahweh won out, and the myth, at least in some respect, was a tool in the Leviathan battle of ideas. Now that the motives of some of the narrative elements and incidents associated with the text have been revealed, it is necessary to investigate the extra-Biblical material: the results of the exegetical expansion carried out by the Church Fathers and the rabbis. What lies at the etiological root of this puzzling myth? Why was humanity inculpated with this first transgression against God and what does the Adamic myth reveal about the character of humanity's relation to evil and to the sacred? These questions may be answered by examining the later developments of the myth, the speculative writings of the Church Leaders who gave us the concepts of the Fall and Original Sin and the nature of the story as myth.

### Adam, Eve, Evil, and Original Sin

The myth of mankind's Fall has resounded tremendously in western societies and continues to have repercussions. One measure of the cultural significance of a myth may be the pervasiveness of its manifestations in a given culture. For Doty, the story of the Fall of Man can be classified as one of the truly relevant, "culturally important" myths, or rather, as belonging to a category of myth which is representative of "particular societies" and which "reappear[s] repeatedly within various frameworks of the society's oral and written literature and [is] represented thematically in rituals and iconography" (13). Likewise,

J. M. Evans characterized the myth of the Fall as one of the singularly most important myths of the western world when he wrote the following:

> Few stories have worked so powerfully or so continuously on the imagination of Western Man as that of the Fall of Adam and Eve. It has been one of the dominant themes of our theology, literature, and art for nearly two thousand years, the subject of commentaries by every major Christian and Jewish thinker from Philo to Dietrich Bonhoeffer, of poems and plays by writers from Prudentius to Bernard Shaw, and of pictures by artists from the anonymous painter who decorated the crypt of San Gennaro in Naples to Marc Chagall. The reasons for its enduring vitality are many, but perhaps the most potent of them is to be found in its nature as a myth. (9)

Evans adds that the story may be considered myth not only in the "poetic sense" of the term but also in the "strictly anthropological sense;" that is, the story has an intrinsic value outside of its re-creation in literature and art, because it communicates a "certain numinous quality" in its distant characters and supernatural events that gives us the sensation that it is communicating something profound and momentous. It is this quality, says Evans, "the urge to formulate this 'something' in the myth of the Fall of Man that has prompted each new generation of readers to reinterpret the first three chapters of Genesis in terms of its own particular values and experience" (9). What is the exact nature of the "something" that has inspired each generation is more difficult to ascertain. Doty believes that the universality of the themes is the basis of the myth's allure. While consecutive cultures may have effected a re-invigoration of the Adamic story by re-interpreting it according to the social and intellectual necessities of the historical epoch, the most important theme in the story nevertheless remains the association of humanity with evil through the notion of Original Sin.

Curiously enough, the Genesis narrative that became associated with the myth of the Fall says nothing about a fall, nor does it depict a fall. In fact, modern mythographers and scholars from other disciplines agree that the metaphor of the fall is extraneous to the Adamic story.[5] Ricoeur points out that the myth of the Fall is so detached from the Judeo-Christian notion of sin that Adam was virtually ignored by writers of the Old Testament (6). According to Freilich, Eden is not presented as a paradise in the Old Testament; rather, paradise is a "state to which the human form slowly evolves" (212). Likewise, Campbell finds that the primitive examples of the Adamic tale are affirmative of life, in general, showing no evidence of the Fall, Original Sin, or the exile from Paradise (105). Somehow the Fall became the metaphorical expression whereby the experience of the privation of God's sanctifying grace—as brought by the primordial sin—was given concrete form. The idea of a Fall may have evolved in Rabbinical literature and Original Sin was the product of early Christian and especially Augustinian post-Biblical documents. Thus, in any study referring to the Biblical tale of Adam and Eve, the term 'Adamic myth' or 'myth of Adam and Eve' is preferable to the common, however erroneous, "myth of the Fall."

As to when and how these ideas emerged, an exact answer is not forthcoming. What may have begun as an innocuous or entertaining etiological story which attempted to justify monogamy, male dominance, the need for work, and/or woman's role as bearer of children (Evans 9), was given the function at some point in time of communicating vital valuational messages: the simple narration was converted into a thesis on evil.[6] This conversion is evident in the Hebrew Bible, the Jewish Apocalyptic literature, in the New Testament and in the extra-Biblical Christian literature of the Early Common Era. Anthony D. York has outlined the influences of these literatures on the figure of Adam in an article that traces the evolution of the figure from Biblical type to literary type. Jewish literature, according to York, is responsible for a drastic change in the role of Adam. The Deuteronomic History (Joshua-Kings) and the prophetic writings (especially those of Jeremiah and Ezekiel) repeatedly emphasized the theme of the Jewish people's oppression and suffering as self-originated. This theme is in line with the proverb of Deuteronomic theology: "good is rewarded and evil is punished; justice prevails. They have been punished; they must be evil." Job introduced a challenge to this dictum by asserting that both good and evil people would be punished: "He destroys blameless and wicked alike" (9:22); and the author of Ecclesiastes, expressed a similar pessimism which he based on the lack of justice in the world: "I saw here under the sun that, where justice ought to be, there was wickedness, and where righteousness ought to be, there was wickedness" (3:16). After the writings of Job and Ecclesiastes, says York, Jewish writers began to look for worldly sources to explain their hardships and the answers were found in the apocalyptic literature of the second century BCE (104-5).

The apocalyptic literature held that the nature of the world itself was evil, so, since evil is opposed to good, these writers had asserted that suffering was not the result of the Jewish people being evil, rather their suffering must be due to the fact that they are a good people in an inherently evil world. By ascribing to this belief, the Jews could substantiate the claim that they were the chosen 'good' people forced to suffer in an evil world. Regarding the question Whence evil?, it was only natural that the rabbis turn to their cosmology, and the enigmatic Genesis 2-3 story was found to be one solution, and the Genesis 6 (where the "son of the gods" were said to have cohabited with "the daughters of men") was another (York 105). The official Jewish theology preferred to adhere to the idea of an "evil imagination" in the first humans, however, the more popular idea of an Adamic basis for evil finally won out with the rabbis (N. P. Williams xiii).

"It is in the application of the Genesis story in this sense," says York, "that we began to get the 'Adam' that is so prominent in western literature" (105). Some of the themes that are common in later literature originate in the Jewish exegetical tradition that treated the theme of Adam and Eve. Satan as the tempter, the fall of the angels, and death as a penalty for Adam's sin are some of the ideas that first emerged in Jewish literature and later became prominent in Christian literary re-creations of the story (York 105).

The concept of Original Sin is notably absent in the writings of the Hebrews. Jewish literature generally teaches, writes York, that death is the penalty for the personal sin of Adam but the sin is not passed on—there is no inherited evil, as in Ezekiel 18:20: "a son shall not share the father's guile, nor a father, his son's" (105—6). In summary, Adam in Jewish literature is the first man, the father of all generations of men who was created as a "second angel" and his body covered all space from heaven to earth; after he sinned, he sank and lost the luminosity which had previously clothed him, and he became naked. One tradition viewed him as androgynous, and Philo believed the story was an allegorical writing in which there were two Adams, a heavenly and an earthly first man (York 106).

When we consider Adam only in light of his role in the Old Testament, it becomes apparent that the figure is relegated a relatively minor significance, for outside of Genesis, Adam is seldom named. Jesus never refers to Adam directly and the figure is only mentioned briefly in the New Testament (Ricoeur 6). Nevertheless, the appropriation of the myth by Jewish and Christian theologians succeeded in converting Adam into one of the most recognizable figures of the Judeo-Christian tradition. The seemingly inconsequential writings of the disciple Paul resuscitated the image of Adam, remolding the figure from its status of mythologized obliquity into an "individualized personage from whom all mankind would be descended physically" (Ricoeur 238). The Christian notion of the history of salvation cast Adam, Humanity, and Christ in a pivotal analogous triangle whereby the beginning, middle, and end of history concretized certain notions of good and evil, of life and death, of paradise lost and found, into one simple, yet profound, theological formula: the first man lived in a garden paradise until he disobeyed God. As a consequence of breaking the rules, all human life would experience suffering until life ended in death. The select people of God would be given everlasting life in the heavenly paradise, while the rest would spend eternity suffering in Hell. In the Christian appropriation of the story of Adam and Eve, according to Evans, the root cause of humanity's nature was established. As Evans points out:

> hereditary sinfulness was declared to be the primary result of Adam's transgression and death the consequent punishment. The Fall implanted in Man an inclination to evil . . . which the Law . . . could reveal but not cure. Only the Grace of God operating through the Atonement could perform the latter function. (60)

In is in the first four centuries of Christianity that the notions of the Fall emerge. The concepts of the Fall and of Original Sin, according to N. P. Williams, were the result in part of the Gnostic syncretistic movement in which Hindu monism and Iranian dualism (theories which suggest the "eternity or necessity of evil") clashed with ideas of a perfect and good god (xvi—xvii). The emphasis on Adam in the Pauline writings raised five issues of importance to the Christian exegetes in the subsequent centuries: (1) was the story intended to be allegorical or historical?; (2) what was the nature of humanity's condition before the Fall—"non-moral innocence, or "Original Righteousness"?; (3) what was the "undesirable thing, state, or quality" which was supposedly passed from Adam to his descendants?; (4) how was this unknown malady transferred from generation to generation?; and (5) what is the "resulting state" of human nature with regards to the future Redemption? In these early years there emerged two basic views of "Fall-doctrine" which corresponded to the Eastern and the western Churches. The first was professed by Origen, who held that the idea of Original Sin as a "weakness rather than a disease, a *privatio* rather than a *depravatio*." The second view, held by Tertullian, the precursor of Augustine, asserted the opposite opinion, that Adam's sin represented a *depravatio*, or a disease (Williams xvi-xviii).

Paul was certainly the first Christian writer to deal with Adam when he considered him as "a type of the one to come" (Romans 5:14). York describes Paul's view of Adam as an "antitype of the Messiah" because Paul's typology is chiefly contrastive. Sin and death are opposed to grace; death is contrasted with resurrection (York 107). Also in the Christian writings, the myth is used to substantiate woman's position in the church, and as a justification of woman's subservience to man. In Mark, the story is used as an example of why monogamy is the preferred form of marriage, as well as the "Jewish theme of the unity of mankind" (York 107).[7]

It is Augustine, however, who has had the most lasting influence on the notions of Adam, Eve, and Original Sin. The predominant view of Adam and his descendants was formulated by the African Bishop into its "classic" form: "the sin of Adam, the cause of his fall, is imputed to his descendants, and they therefore are sinners by nature before they are sinners by deed (York 109). Some of the features of Augustine's belief are that humanity experiences an "original guilt" and a "seminal identity." Original Sin is regarded as a "depravation" rather than as a "privation" and concupiscence is considered as intrinsically evil (Williams xx). Augustine also believed that humanity's free will was destroyed as a result of Adam's actions which were motivated by a "desire for independence, for freedom of the will, [which] was itself, paradoxically, the root of sin" (York 109).

In addition to Augustine, Origen, Tertullian, and Ambrose also wrote of the transmission of the sin of Adam to his descendants. Although these writers concentrated on ascertaining the nature of the first sin and the effects it had on humanity, other questions occupied their minds as well, and the "fascination with Adam as the newly minted man led many of these writers to ask very detailed questions" (York 110). Indeed the historical nature of the characters was reaffirmed by these writings. Any question as to the existence of Adam, that Adam had been a historical man was settled after Augustine. In this new role opposite Christ, the Adamic figure was ultimately transformed from *adam* (the Hebrew common noun) to Adam. The figure was given historical life; and in the words of Ricoeur, "Christology consolidated Adamology," hence the "demythologization of the Adamic figure" (238). A figure which had existed in an oral medium, which had been poised on the brink between historical fact and mythological uncertainty, was given a factual identity by the Hebrew and Christian writers: 'man' and 'woman' who transgressed against the too-human God became the first man and the first woman, guilty of the first sin which by heredity indicted all humans.

The results of the Jewish patriarchs' interpretation of Adam's disobedience as the birth of evil in humankind had enormous consequences. Perhaps it is a testament to the portentous power of language, that a simple narrative has so charged the conscience of a religious tradition, that the excessive weight of centuries of exegesis and overt promotion of a simple idea—that humanity is inherently evil—has spawned an entire culture of guilt and fear around it. There is no doubt that the notions of the Fall and Original Sin provided an incendiary spark to the fires of Christian fanaticism. We will never know, writes Ricoeur, the lives that have perished due to the literal reading of this tale, its confusion with history, and especially the Augustinian conclusions about Original Sin (239). Yet for all the darker consequences of this notion of human evil, the idea of an original sin and the narrative that came to embody it also inspired some of the world's great artistic works. In all of these processes—the appropriation and evolution of the ancient myth, its more than twenty centuries of exegetical analysis, its depiction in artistic forms, the reduction of the figures from charac-ter in dramatic narrative to static symbols in Christian art, literature, and theol-ogy—the figures of Adam and Eve, the myth, and the extra-textual elements derived from the speculative writings became ingrained into the western psyche. In Spain, the myth, the figures and their ideological sub-texts would continue to be culturally significant well into the nineteenth century.

# Chapter Two:

## Adam and Eve in the Spanish Dramatic Tradition

Throughout the history of Christianity, artistic representations have functioned as a means of dissemination of the Church's system of beliefs. Paintings, engravings, and in later centuries, dramatic pieces were essential utilitarian media in the divulgence of Biblical and doctrinal ideas such as the annunciation and the birth of Christ, the crucifixion and the resurrection. The Genesis narrative became the model for poets of the fourth and fifth centuries who worked the story into epic and dramatic forms; the earliest known text in a Romance language being the *Jeu d'Adam*, dating from the twelfth century. In Spain, the Adamic *autos* were performed as a part of the annual Corpus Christi celebration. Set before an audience that was curious about its beginnings, the Adamic story in dramatic form was a necessary product of the Renaissance culture, where, according to Arnold Williams, the production and consumption of the speculative material related to this creation story had become common intellectual fare, reaching its zenith during the fifteenth and sixteenth centuries in Europe (6). Before looking specifically at some of the Spanish Adamic plays, it is necessary to understand the ideological environment of Europe in general, and of the Iberian Peninsula specifically, during the early modern period from which the Adamic *autos* and the *comedias* emerged.

In his detailed study of the Genesis Commentaries, A. Williams notes that it is difficult for the student of European culture to comprehend the Renaissance without taking into consideration the enormous importance given to the Book of Genesis. Although Greek and Roman materials and models provided much inspiration, the "habit of mind was predominantly theological" (3); thus, in the roughly one-hundred-year period from 1525 to 1633, European presses produced over forty commentaries on the Book of Genesis (6). The artistic texts began in the fourth and fifth centuries, but the sixteenth and seventeenth centuries represent the period of highest output of Genesis related texts in the modern languages.[1] The "meaningful history" communicated by the Genesis B story, the theological notion of the Original Sin, and the use of Adam and Eve as the most notable symbols for this conceptual framework, would reach a peak of cultural significance during this time. Not only were the commentaries on the creation and the artistic works theological tools, but the notion of the loss of the primal paradisiacal state and the subsequent degenerative evils bestowed on humans through genetic inheritance reflected, in part, the greater Weltansicht that characterized much of the European Renaissance.

In his study of the pessimistic tenor of Europe during the sixteenth and seventeenth centuries, Jean Delumeau notes that the notion of Original Sin influenced all theological commentary and its "diverse by-products—problems of grace, of free will or servitude, of predestination" came to be "prime obsessions" of the Europeans (248). Delumeau regards this intense interest in sin as par with the spirit of "dominant pessimism" during the Renaissance where "[t]he appeal of the macabre, the sense that the world was going from bad to worse, and the conviction that humanity is fragile . . . left a deep imprint on the culture of the time" (189).

The author goes on to relate this intense awareness of Original Sin with a similar notion immensely popular during this period, namely, the myth of the Golden Age. This timeless myth of an other-worldly epoch, devoid of human want and suffering, and replete with bounty to the contentment of all, was revived in the writings of the Christian fathers, Ambrose and Augustine, who interpreted the tale as a paganization of the Biblical Eden (255-256), thus establishing a symmetrical relationship between Adam's Original Sin and the Golden Age. As the early modern Europeans contemplated the poverty, famine, wars, and disease around them, images of peace, of plenty, of healthful youth, filled their minds in an attempt to reverse the harshness of reality: utopian fantasies, images of the mysterious and plentiful Orient, dreams of El Dorado, the fountain of youth, and especially the promise of regaining paradise through the voyages to the new world. According to Delumeau, the belief in paradise "reinforced" its opposite—the belief in the Fall: "the more the first sin was made ugly, the more the pre-lapsarian state was embellished, and vice versa" (257-258). Citing further evidence of the West's insistence on human guilt, the effects of sin, the need to fear God, and a widespread deprecation of the world, Delumeau's final point is well made: in the realm of theology, the Renaissance's new-found interest in humanism was not optimistic (556).

If the general theological pessimism contributed to the belief in the Adamic notion of paradise lost, the theological struggles of the era would situate the figure of Adam and the doctrine of Original Sin at the heart of the Church's defense of its belief and ritual system. According to N. P. Williams, the Reformation gave the ideas of the Fall and Original Sin a "new lease on life," for it

had the remarkable effect of dragging the doctrines . . . out from the cloister and the lecture-room into the market-place, of making them issues of the greatest interest and importance for the religious life of hundreds of thousands of ordinary people. (419)

Martin Luther held a pessimistic view of Adam's sin, believing that human nature had been so corrupted by Adam's actions that the will had become ineffectual in human salvation. As Karen Armstrong has pointed out, Luther believed that "good works" and the "observance of the Law" are not the cause of salvation, rather the result (277). In order to check the spread of Protestant ideas, the Church now had to apply a more rigorous conformity than before and a "greater degree of vigilance" regarding religious dissent (Elliot 214). The idea of Adam's sin became official with the specification of its characteristics in written form. Only then could the Roman Church counter the Protestant schism. The Council of Trent met for the first time in 1545, and then in 1547, where an attempt was made to define the pre-lapsarian and post-lapsarian natures of Adam, the nature of the first parents' sin and of the "fallen" condition passed through the generations, and finally, the remedies for this "tainted" condition (N. P. Williams 420). From this period forward, the doctrine of Original Sin would become an official tool in the intellectual struggle signifying that salvation depended on the will and the actions of the faithful.

It was only natural that the theologians return to the Adamic myth for the justification of salvation through the acts of the will. The notion of Evil was never ambiguous to the Europeans, because, in the words of Delumeau, to an "entire civilization, Original Sin had become a sort of *deus ex machina*, constantly used as the final and definitive reason for all that goes bad in the universe" (253). Adam, the myth, and the adjunct notions defining Original Sin had become a part of the West's transcendental cultural signs, pointing beyond time and beyond history to the mythic world of no-time: the beginning. It is this atemporal point of nothing-before where the vision of the inherent corruption of humanity, the vision that contributed to the general pessimism in the Christian cultures, should have its start. This is also the place to which the vision of the world as redeemable would have to return.

If these statements ring true for Europe in general, what then of the topically austere conservatism of Spain where, according to J. H. Elliott, the humanist tradition gave way to an ever growing "religious dogmatism" (217)? There were more practical reasons for concentrating the Spanish public's attention on Adam and his sin, not the least of which were Spain's history of conquest, the heterogeneous religious and racial make-up of society, the Counter-Reformation, the ignorance of religion on the part of the masses, and lastly, a humanist curiosity for the history and beginnings of the world. After

Granada had been reconquered, and after the forced conversion of the Spanish Jews, the sudden rise of Lutheranism became the new threat to the Roman Church and to Spain as its staunch defender. The nation was experiencing a new sense of spiritual intensity, evident in the reform movements of the religious orders and in the creation of seventeen new orders (Elliott 243). It was this renewed spirit of conquest in the spiritual realm which would culminate in the reign of Philip II, projecting itself as the bulwark and the citadel of the Christian faith in the world.

Thus, to the Roman Church, the Adamic plays were an enormously significant audio-visual tool used for the education of a populace that was, to a large part, ignorant of the Christian tenets. Of primary concern to the clergy was the "Christianization" of the Spanish people, most of whom were not knowledgeable in the most basic Christian truths (Dedieu 1-2), and who lived in rural areas with limited exposure to orthodox practices (Kamen 199-200). Even the Inquisition which had originally focused on heresy, shifted its attention to Old Christians when it was discovered that "in many parts of Spain, it could be doubted whether there was any true religion at all" (Kamen 198-199). Given the scope of the problem, it was necessary that the Church use a means that would communicate to the greatest number of people. The illiteracy rate reached as high as eighty percent and there were two means available to those people who could not read or write: illiterates could participate in the culture of written letters through the reading of the written text (Beverly 219), or they could view the drama, one of the most effective and popular forms of mass communication in Spain's Golden Age.

### Adam and Eve in the *auto sacramental*

In the hands of the dramatists, the Genesis B narration was a ready-made tale of universal conflict between Good and Evil, with humanity at the center of the duel. Regarding the relation between drama and theology, and humanity as the axis between good and evil, Gabriel González has written that the overall theme of the baroque theater is "el hombre como campo de acción de dos fuerzas contrarias que hacen de su vida una situación conflictiva permanente" (50). What better example of this dramatic scheme than the Biblical tale where the archetypal pattern is first presented: perfect order and total harmony are toppled due to the introduction of a possible evil, and an ill-made exercise of human will. Nevertheless, there were certain problems that had to be worked out regarding the Biblical narrative, the adjunct doctrinal precepts, and the dramatization of these events and ideas on stage. Not only were the dramatists writing a reenactment of an historical event that included cosmic, human, and supernatural elements, but the Genesis B text was replete with narrative gaps and unmotivated action and dialogue. Representations of God and the serpent, the notion of the pre-lapsarian paradisiacal eden, the state of original innocence that endowed the first humans with faculties beyond the human norm, and motivations for unusual actions would challenge the imagination of the most adept dramatist.

The Adamic myth appears first in Renaissance drama in the cyclical mystery and morality plays performed for the celebration of Corpus Christi where the nature and the focus of these plays, according to Donald T. Dietz, were the three "advents" of God into the affairs of humanity: namely, the creation, the redemption, and the forthcoming judgment (74). The "miracle-mystery" plays dramatized Old Testament accounts, the lives of Saints, and Christ; while the morality plays tended to "allegorize the vices and virtues and pit good against evil." The English Corpus Christi cycle was principally concerned with the "miracle-mystery" play, while the Spanish eucharistic tradition incorporated both the miracle plays and the morality plays (Dietz 79). The *autos* were a part of the Christian liturgy, which is defined by Arias as the "prayers, sermons, songs, gestures, and ceremonies [that] are understood and used as signs, . . . [which] point to a reality of a higher order" (20). These were generally related by theme to the celebration of the doctrine of the Eucharist.[2]

The representative plays chosen for this study are taken from the *Códice de autos viejos* (1578),[3] and are indicative of these two stylistic variants, the mystery and morality types. The *Aucto de los hierros de Adán* and the *Farsa del sacramento de Adán* are allegorical plays in which a new plot has been created utilizing allegorical characters which were considered essential elements of the Genesis story and the doctrinal precepts it was intended to convey. On the other hand, the *Aucto del peccado de Adán* and the *Aucto de la prevaricación de nuestro padre Adán* are mostly non-allegorical works where the narrative elements are similar to those of the Genesis B myth, and where allegorical figures are minimal. The selection of these plays is not meant to be all-inclusive. There are other autos, especially of the allegorical variety, which deal with Adam, Original Sin, and the Last Judgment.[4] For the purposes of this study however, I have chosen four works that are closely related to the Genesis B; whereas many of the allegorical autos deal with the moral condition of man and are only concerned with the figure of Adam in its most general symbol of the first man as representative of Humankind.

Perhaps nowhere within the tradition of the eucharistic drama in Spain is the mixture of allegorical and "historical" representation, of morality and mystery types, more evident than in the group of *autos* that treat the mythical characters Adam and Eve. This stylistic duality may reflect the theologians' desire to express distinct meanings regarding the Adamic figure: on the one hand an representation of the Genesis story by the non-allegorical pieces that closely follow the Biblical story (the mystery type); as opposed to the expression of Original Sin which would be expressed in the morality play, the allegorical pieces that create new plots. Speaking of the *auto* in general, Wardropper has commented on the intent of the plays when he states that the plays "tradujeron las sutilezas teológicas a términos cotidianos" (110), and that the dramatization of Christian tenets was made especially effective by incorporating allegorical expression into the works (105). Pérez Priego sees the relation between the dogma and its expression in the *autos* as being more narrowly linked, when he writes: "[p]or cuanto se refiere a lo conceptual, las obras del *Códice* contienen, más que una mera exposición, una proclamación estricta de la doctrina católica más ortodoxa" (37). On the other hand, Arias does not consider the content of the plays as being restricted necessarily to Christian doctrine:

> Writers of autos and spiritual writers in general do not always follow the strict interpretations of the liturgical signs. They very often show a considerable amount of freedom and indeed ingenuity in the interpretation of signs, things, and events. This tendency goes back to the beginning of the Christian era; it flourished during the Middle Ages, and in Spain it continued to the end of the Golden Age. (21)

The doctrinal intent of the morality or allegorical *autos* with their creative plots and characters seem more obvious: to teach the principles of Original Sin. But what about the pieces that re-created the Genesis B story? In the Genesis there is no mention of paradise; there is nothing about a Fall, no original state of perfection that was lost, and there is no idea of inherited sin. The dramatists had to write these notions into the non-allegorical pieces in order to teach the doctrine of Original Sin.

Despite the plethora of Genesis material circulating during the Renaissance, and the failure of the Church to express in unambiguous terms the nature of Adam and his sin even within the Council of Trent,[5] these short pieces reflect considerable unanimity in their interpretation of Adam and Eve. Generally, the figures, like most of the characters in the *autos*, were reduced to abstractions or types. Adam was depicted as a symbol of humanity's sin and as the analogical opposite of Christ. These are the symbolical values that are most manifest to scholars who have considered these works and their role within the corpus of *autos*. In his introduction to the *Códice de autos viejos*, Pérez Priego mentions the singularity of the Adamic *autos* for focusing on Adam as a sign of humanity's separation from God and eventual reunion with God by means of Christ:

> . . . son las piezas sobre la figura de Adán, que . . . constituyen una categoría independiente y original en el *Códice*, las que concentran mucho más eficazmente aquella idea dramática, en cuanto que Adán supone el punto de unión entre la vieja y la nueva ley y en él se encierra todo el proceso de la rendención del género humano. . . . No sorprende, pues, que en esas obras se ponga ya en marcha el procedimiento alegórico que transforma a Adán en el personaje del Hombre que será redimido por Cristo en el sacramento. (35-36)

In a similar vein, Wardropper, in his study of the evolution of the early *auto sacramental*, groups the Adamic works with the Resurrection plays (221), pointing out the significance of Adam, especially as the character pertains to the use of allegorical language to express the "abstract" tenets of the Church:

> Este papel universalizado lo desempeña Adán en muchos autos del *Códice*. Nada más con cambiar el nombre de Adán por El Hombre se podría regularizar la alegoría. Este proceso tuvo lugar en la época misma del *Códice*. Si en *Los hierros de Adán* es posible tomar el papel de Adán por el del Hombre, en algunos Hombres se traslucen los rasgos personales y los detalles biográficos del Adán histórico y tradicional. En esta transición dramática consiste el *trait d'union* buscado por los críticos. En el personaje que representa la Humanidad. . . . Es evidente que estos autores de estas obras comprendían perfectamente la importancia de su tratamiento de Adán. (233)

Whenever the sacraments are represented as a literary theme, continues Wardropper, there is a tendency to use the same literary construct as the theological treatments, namely allegory (104). The role of allegory in the *autos* is to make "plástica y visible" the structure of the Christian dogma. If the public could not comprehend intellectually the abstract tenets of the dogma, it could certainly understand "tangible objects and theatrical characters" (Wardropper

110). It is no surprise then that the characteristic that most distinguishes Adam in the allegorical plays is this composite nature. Adam is the allegorical figure "por excelencia" according to Louise Fothergill-Payne, because from within the figure one may discover multiple secondary values related to the whole. In the *auto* Adam becomes:

> el ser *sintético*, es decir, que él solo representa y encierra en sí mismo todos los demás conceptos encarnados en los personajes secundarios. Estos, en efecto, no son más que sus *alterego*. El protagonista alegórico, por su conducta y pensamiento, crea a los demás personajes, que existen sólo gracias a él. Este es su rasgo esencialmente dramático: su soledad y su responsabilidad de vivir su propio mundo, creando y recreándolo por un solo acto, traspié o cambio de parecer. A medida que se suceden los acontecimientos en la escena, éstos van revelando más aspectos suyos y todos estos juntos constituyen el carácter del protagonista. Al mismo tiempo, aislando estos aspectos como personajes secundarios, el alegorista les da vida propia como personificaciones de una idea con las múltiples posibilidades inherentes a cada una de ellas. (33)

Thus, we find that the *Aucto de los hierros de Adán* presents "figuras" such as Libre Albedrío, El Deseo, La Ygnorancia and El Trabajo, as the cohorts and children of Padre Adán. The allegorical characters are drawn as *pícaros* who argue, swear, and blame one another for instigating the fatal sin that has left them "exiled," "imprisoned," "sad," "afflicted" and ignorant. The simple conflict centers on these characters, these components of Padre Adán, who complain of their negative conditions, all of which are derived from the first sin. A resolution is set forth by the introduction of La Sabiduría, Fee, Esperança, Charidad, and La Misericordia,— representing the opposite camp—who become the guides and protectors of Adam's children, leading them to God's ways, announcing the coming of Christ, and effecting an evolution in their character.

The sum of the composite characters and their actions—the bantering and accusations among Adam's "children"—present the first man as a comical rustic, incapable of controlling his desires: "pues por una golosina / tanto herraje traes" (219). The introduction of El Herror (a stage note informs that this is El Demonio) as a temptor also provides moments of humor; however, the message is not intended to be frivolous. The notion of humanity's shared sin is emphasized from the beginning of the piece by the use of a *villancico*, sung by Adam and his children, and by a soliloquy delivered afterward by Padre Adán, both of which highlight the negative consequences of the sin for the first man and for humanity:

> Triste viene el padre Adan
> y los que con el andamos,
> triste viene y tristes vamos.
>    Triste esta por la maliçia
> con que a su Dios ofendio,
> y tanbien porque perdio
> su graçia, paz y amiçiçia.
> Castiganos la justiçia,
> misericordia esperamos;
> triste viene y tristes vamos. (216)

In these first lines, the ruptured relationship between humanity and God is evident as well as the wickedness attributed to Adam. In an opening soliloquy, Adam recounts his story in Paradise, reducing the tale to its most essential details: Paradise is a "canpo damaçeno, / lugar de tanta esçelencia" and Adam's pre-lapsarian condition is defined as "ygnocençia" and "santo y bueno." Adam admits that he sinned because of "gula" and "cobdiçia," and that afterward he found himself "en neçesidad, / muerto de sed y hanbriento, / ciego de la voluntad, / neçio del entendimiento" (217). Not surprisingly, this *auto* uses the word *hierros* in its title, both as a pun and a metaphor, signifying Adam's fallen condition, and also pointing out the physical circumstances in which he is portrayed: because of his *hierros*, Adam is fettered in irons to El Trabajo, manifesting in visible action and rhetorical conceits the notion that humanity is bound to its sinful nature in its hereditary relationship to the first man.

In another allegorical piece, *Farsa del sacramento de Adán*, the figure of Adam is presented as a father who must seek sustenance for his children, Apetito Sensitivo and Apetito Racional. Here the allegorist draws the figure in accordance with the Biblical idea of the dual nature of humanity: that Adam was made of matter and endowed with a spirit. The conflict between flesh and spirit affects humanity's judgment, because it is believed that the faculty of reason is impeded by the appetites of the body. Although the Genesis B did not present this dualistic conflict in either Adam nor Eve, the early Church Fathers' emphasis on free will assured that the conflict between desire and reason was imposed on the Adamic figure and its conceptual paradigm. The first sin, then, was seen as an early model for the motif of "reason pandering to will" or desire, and this opposition became a commonplace in the literature of love (Green 197).

While there are allusions to the notions of the transgression: "[e]ra yo favorecido / del que los cielos formó . . . Todo cuanto hubo criado / lo subjetó a mi mandado, / mas ya convirtió el contento / en un amargo tormento / aquel acerbo bocado" (175), the focus of the play is on the salvation by Christ in the Eucharist. When Ley de Gracia and Fe appear, the message of the redemption is announced and the presence of Christ in the "divino manjar" is explained to the public.

In both the allegorical plays, Adam and his complimentary characters function to varying degrees as symbolic reminders of the notion of the primal sin and the need to rectify it through faith in God's grace. The *Aucto de los hierros de Adán* is primarily concerned with the expression of the negative conditions that afflict humanity because of the first sin, while the *Farsa del sacramento de Adán* presents the conflict of reason and desire, as a condition of the first sin for which faith in the saving grace of the Eucharist is the solution. The references to Paradise, extraneous to the Book of Genesis, serve to heighten the notion of loss due to the breach. The messages of salvation are the *deus ex machina* that resolves the simple conflicts linking Adam/humanity with Christ. The message of humanity's flawed condition and the means to rectify this state are not elaborated beyond the most simple schemes presented by the abstract characters, their afflictions, and the positive characters who represent the redeeming attributes of the Church's sacraments.

On the other hand, the *autos* that dramatize the Genesis B story are automatically more complicated than the allegorical pieces in terms of plot development and character, no doubt due to the nature of the Genesis B narrative. The authors of the *Aucto del peccado de Adán* and the *Aucto de la prevaricación de nuestro padre Adán* had to deal with some of the particular uncertainties with which earlier dramatists of the Adamic myth were confronted: "[q]uestions of continuity and character [as well as] narrative and metaphysical" problems required, in the words of J. Evans, "the constant invention of both speech and incident" (192-193). Adam and Eve in these non-allegorical pieces would not merely mimic the Bible story's characters; instead, Adam and Eve were essential in establishing the dramatic correlation of many of the Biblically extraneous precepts of the doctrine of Original Sin.

In the *Aucto del peccado de Adán*, as in the Biblical narration, Adam plays a diminished role. The action of the piece revolves around the temptation of Eve by Luçifer (in a snake costume) and his helpers Gula, and Avariçia; God's condemnation of the serpent and the people; and finally the exile of the first couple. The expression of pre-lapsarian innocence and of Paradise are given to Adam, whose opening speech about the humans' gratitude to God reflects a common practice in other dramatizations of this scene: "rriquezas sin quento" and "esta potençia / del muy alto entendimiento, / para que, a Dios entendiendo, / con la voluntad le amemos" (133). Paradise is a garden of odiferous flowers, fruit trees, plants, and grasses. Besides exceptional understanding, the first couple possesses "almas linpias y puras," (134).

This first man is an obedient husband who willingly tastes the fruit to avoid the threats of anger by Eve, the stronger of the two. Although Adam admits that it is "grande ynpedimento / la soberana jusion / y el divino mandamiento," he obeys his wife's command to eat when she says: "pues que yo e mordido; / no me hagas enojar" (140). When confronted by God, this Adam, like his Biblical counterpart, blames Eve—"y ella me hiço comer"—however, he differs in that he claims that he did it to please her. Adam's actions and dialogue reflect an indulgent and resigned personality. The condemnation scene follows where God curses the three perpetrators and Adam accepts humbly God's justice for his actions. Later, exiled by God, Adam asks an Angel for a sign of alleviation. Having received news of "la suma Clemencia" and a future pardon, he again admits his guilt and resigns himself to labor in penitence until he might be forgiven (148-49).

The *Aucto de la prevaricación de nuestro padre Adán*, according to Pérez Priego, may have been penned by Micael De Carvajal (c.1501-c.1576) (146), and the piece represents the most skillful depiction of the Genesis B in the Adamic *autos*. Again, Adán is more concerned with pleasing Eva than with offending God: "[p]or hacelle complacer . . . lo he gustado" (158),—there is no attempt to take avantage of a potentially dramatic moment. Adán offers no resistance to Eve's request to eat. The play opens with Adam's description of Paradise, which is a bountiful land where nature serves the needs of the first humans:

> Hizo el cielo tan dotado
> d'estrellas y de planetas;
> pues el aire, tan poblado
> de avecicas, y habitado,
> a nuestro querer subjetas.
>   Los pescados en el mar
> y las fieras en la tierra
> hizo por nos sustentar;
> púsolo a nuestro mandar,
> que nada nos hace guerra.
>   Los cielos dan movimientos

sólo por nos conservar,
las estrellas influimentos,
y también los elementos
nos sirven sin descansar:
el fuego nos tiempla el frío,
el aire defiende el fuego,
el agua con su rocío
a la sed quita su brío,
la tierra nos da sosiego.
Mira, pues, el alegría
del sol, también de la luna:
cómo el sol alumbra el día,
la luna la noche unbría;
todos nos sirven a una. (147-148)

This idealization of the elements of nature where nothing threatens the human pair is emphasized by the dramatist so that the loss of this "[l]ugar de contentamiento" may form an effective contrast between the pre-lapsarian and post-lapsarian states. The loss of God's favor and of Paradise are not the only negative effects of the "Fall" presented in this piece. After the pair are expelled from the garden, the dramatist quickly shifts his focus from the Genesis scene into the historical present and the Spanish public, as Adán muses to humanity about his role in history:

¡Oh humana naturaleza,
cuánto te he menoscabado!
Despojéte tu riqueza,
dejéte en suma probeza [sic],
púsete en mortal estado.
Toda la humana nación
se queje del mal Adán,
pues cometí tal traición
que vendí toda creación
y la subjeté a Satán. (164-165)

The author of this *auto*, in contrast to the previously mentioned piece, focuses more on the consequences of Adam's sin for humanity; nevertheless, this notion is countered by placing sin as a part of the master plan, thus lessening the severity of the transgression. In a speech directed to Eve, Adam is shown to be the first prophet announcing Christ, thus mitigating the severity of his crime:

Cuando deste mi costado
Dios Padre a ti te formaba,
en aquel sueño pesado
allí me fue revelado
un secreto que ordenaba:
   y es que había de encarnar
su hijo en nuestra nación;
esto me hace esperar
qu'este divino abajar
es por nuestra redención. (461-470)

If the critics have focused on the basic role of Adam as sinner in these plays, it is because the playwrights followed the exegets by interpreting Adam and Eve as theological symbols of Original Sin and not as historical entities. The basic concepts associated with the Adamic figure in Christian dogma, the group of ideas that make up the conceptual paradigm of Original Sin, were given concrete form in the *auto* to the degree that each contributed to the didactic message of the piece, and no attempt was made to portray Adam and Eve as anything more than basic symbols in the Christian equation: Adam and Eve equals humanity equals sin. This equation was resolved by the formula: Christ equals redemption from sin. The *autos* of Renaissance Spain, were essentially a continuation of a Medieval tradition, and the figure of Adam portrayed in these short plays was a product of the Medieval mentality, which, according to Ernst Cassirer, "tries to spin a thick web of analogies over the entire cosmos and to capture the whole physical and spiritual world in the network of these analogies" (88). Arias, speaking of the non-allegorical pieces, expresses his opinion that the *autos* present some of their most expressive moments and the makings of "excellent drama" when the rebellion of man is unfolded, then resolved in the Christian message of eternal salvation (26). I do not believe that this statement applies to the Adamic *autos*, where the conflict in the pieces never moves beyond the most facile oppositional plane. This limited portrayal of Adam would change when the professional playwrights began writing Adam and his tale into longer dramatic works.

### Adam and Eve in the *comedia nueva*

With the tenets of the Catholic church under siege in the fifteenth century, Adam and Eve had become important symbols for the dissemination of the doctrine of Original Sin and in the preservation of the orthodox Church. The representation of Adam as a symbol of Original Sin and as the analogical opposite of Christ had been the focus of the allegorical Adamic *autos*, these Adamic themes also became the subject of the national drama. In the hands of Lope de Vega and of Luis Vélez de Guevara y Dueñas, the creation story was expanded into the popular three-act *comedia nueva*, which because of its longer structure would require more creative manipulation of the Creation myth, as well as the addition of other material taken from other chapters of the Book of Genesis. Now the dramatists could continue the Biblical story by treating Adam and Eve in exile, by including the tale of Cain and Abel, and thus allowing the dramatists to represent the effects of the first sin on subsequent generations. Vélez de Guevara's *La creación del mundo*, written around the first decades of the seventeenth century, and Lope's *La creación del mundo y primera culpa del hombre*, from the same period, filled in the gaps of the terse Biblical story with expanded dialogue, action, and characters not found in the Genesis. Each playwright created his own interpretation of the Biblical stories, and in Lope's Adamic play, the depiction of Adam and Eve as symbols would give way to a more realistic representation of the first humans as historical people.

Speaking about dramatic characters in a speech entitled *Personaje y abstracción*, Domingo Ynduráin stated that in the Spanish *auto* and the *comedia* of the Golden Age, there is a tendency to present characters as types or abstractions, instead of as individual characters that represent a "reflejo de la realidad" (28-36). This is an often debated question among the scholars who study the *comedia*, for within the corpus of many of Spain's playwrights, one may find arguments for and against this notion. It is logical to assume that the implantation of a Biblical type into the *comedia* would produce new analogies, new meanings that would enhance the hitherto restricted figure of Adam. Given that the Biblical model for each play in this study was the same (both treat the creation in the first act, the story of Cain and Abel in the second, and the fate of Cain in the third), the manner in which each playwright treated the Genesis creation material produced a remarkably distinct characterization of the Biblical characters. Vélez de Guevara, whose historical and religious dramas enjoyed notoriety, followed closely the narrative segments of the Biblical text, and as a consequence, produced characters that are shallow, little more than the figures previously represented in the *autos*. While his work was mostly imitative, certain allegorical and supernatural elements were added to the Biblical stories to enhance the didactic function of the plays. On the other hand, Lope de Vega's presented a more imaginative interpretation of the Genesis stories, achieving a representation of the narrative that required few supernatural elements to distract from the humanistic focus of his play. The result was a portrayal of Adam and Eve that revealed the signature of Lope as an artist and was singular in Spain's dramatic tradition.

In their introduction to Luís Vélez de Guevara's, *La creación del mundo*, Henryk Ziomek and Robert White Linker describe Vélez de Guevara's characters as "quite human," modeled on the Spanish rural laborers "who feel Nature with much energy, almost identifying themselves with the land they work" (17). In addition, Adam is found to be the "perfect accord of the Spanish peasant," for he is shown as contented and in no way a threat to the order of society: "humble, and subdued" (17). Nevertheless, Vélez de Guevara's Adam never really evolves beyond the symbolic type presented in the *autos*. Adam is presented as humble, yet not contented; a laborer, yes, but not in harmony with the land.

Vélez de Guevara's Adam is limited in the first act in the same way that Adam is a limited personage in the Genesis. Adam is mostly silent in the Bible, and thus, Vélez de Guevara gives his first man few speeches. This Adam is portrayed mainly as the pious and obedient servant, timid in God's presence, and answering God's commands with humbleness and subordination. In the first speech of the play, when Dios Padre informs the new man of the nature of the heavens and the earth, Adam's sententious response demonstrates the correct attitude, that of acknowledging his reverence and humility before God: "Criador eterno de todo, / todas las cosas se mueban / para alabar tu grandeça / . . . / y yo, de tierra formado, / . . . / a comprender no alcanço / una parte de ti apenas" (65). Adam's relationship with Eve is another example where Vélez de Guevara respects the brevity of the Genesis narration. Upon seeing Eve, Adam's words closely imitate his speech in Genesis, chapter two: "esta muger ella es huesso de los mis huessos[;]" nevertheless, Guevara adds these words, suggesting, in a somewhat modest manner, the bonds of sexual love that man and woman will share:

> ¡A güeso
> de mis güesos, carne bella
> de mi carne, ermosa ymagen,
> çifra de naturaleça!
> Por ésta dejará el honbre

> su padre y madre, y con tiernas
> muestras de amar de sus braços
> hará hermosas cadenas. (28)

Regarding the depiction of Adam, the similarity of this speech to the Biblical text reveals the author's almost painstaking adherence to the original. While the *autos* tended to focus the action on the four characters: Adam, Eve, Lucifer and God; Vélez de Guevara places more emphasis on Dios Padre and on Luzbel. Dios Padre is a character derived from a combination of Jahweh and the Sky God, for he is a physical presence in the scene, acting alongside his creatures. However, in his speech he possesses the more serious transcendence of the God of Genesis A. After Dios Padre tells the humans of the admonition, the scene shifts to Luzbel, who, with the fallen angels Astarot, Berçebú and Satanás, plots vengeance on the humans. Rather than attempt to portray the temptations of Eve by the serpent, and of Adam by Eve, Vélez de Guevara places the narration of these actions in the words of Astarot, who recounts how he deceived the woman by taking the form of the serpent. Finally, adhering to the Biblical text, our dramatist presents God's search for Adam and Eve, and his condemnation of the humans along with the serpent. When they are exiled by an angel, this Adán replies with resignation that the "castigo a sido justo, / pues ofendimos los dos" (38). Because of Vélez de Guevara's rather strict adherence to the Genesis text, the character of Adam does not achieve any depth beyond the most basic symbolic notion of transgressor against God.

With the presentation of Cain and Abel in the second and third acts, Vélez de Guevara continues this insistence on the chief role of Adam as sinner. The post-lapsarian Adam of act two alludes frequently to the first sin and its punishment. He laments to Eve the difficulty of laboring for food, and the loss of Paradise. When Cain brings an apple to dinner, Adam tells him about the sin, later recounting to his children the entire history of the Creation and the Fall. There is no justification for the decision to sin, only the idea of self-deception by desire:

> Y engañados y bençidos
> de nuestro mismo deseo,
> al fin del fruto comimos.
> Echónos Dios de su graçia,
> como de su parayso,
> viniendo a estos yermos canpos
> desnudos y peregrinos,

> donde por la ynobediençia
> viniendo de Dios malditos,
> de nuestro sudor comemos
>
> . . .
>
> hasta que llegue la muerte. (61-62)

When Cain asks for an explanation of death, Adam clarifies that death is, "de nuestra culpa castigo / justamente pronunçiado" (62), showing that this character is destined to suffer with resignation God's castigation until his death in act three.

In addition to the supernatural characters Dios Padre, Lusbel, and the fallen angels, this play is not without an array of allegorical figures. In order to point out the necessary patrimony between Adam and humanity, the figure Tienpo arrives at the end of act one to inform the humans that they will produce all the races of the world; and Muerte reminds the humans (and the Spanish public) that it is because of the first sin that all generations of humans will die (44-47). After the first couple has suffered their labor in repentance, Amor passes along the message that they not lose hope, because "el Amor Divino, / [puede] bençer en el pleyto / la justiçia de Dios mismo" and the son of God will come to take them from limbo (66). While this play is more elaborate than the *autos*, the essential message of Vélez de Guevara's representation of the first four chapters of Genesis is the same. The murder of Abel by Cain is shown to be an extension of the sin of the first parents, and Adam fulfills the role of father of humanity and instigator of sin. While the playwright's close imitation did not produce any significant modification in the characters of Adam and Eve, it may be said that Vélez de Guevara only created a more elaborated type, or figure, instead of a character based upon more individual attributes. This conclusion would concur with the observation of C. George Peale, that Vélez did not write this piece as a *comedia* for the stage, rather as a *comedia de repente*, a skeleton script used by poets who improvised on a well-known text as a form of diversion (140). It is no wonder that the genius of Lope, using the same model, would create a dramátic character possessed of an individuality betraying characteristics that would remind us not of Adam as literary type, but rather, Adam as the "historical" man.

In a detailed study of Lope's *La creación del mundo y primera culpa del hombre* (1618), Edward Glaser has shown that the prolific dramatist, instead of adhering to the first four chapters of the Book of Genesis, drew freely upon extra-Biblical material in order to tell a unified story of the first parents' sin, and its subsequent consequences for humanity: "corruption and death to all [Adam and Eve's] descendants" through the action of Cain's murder of Abel (55). Concentrating primarily on theological premises, Glaser successfully argues that Lope's Biblical play is more than a simple reenactment of humanity's first transgression: the play's "meaning" resides in its expression of the theological message of Christianity's "promise of life eternal" (32).

Glaser's evidence for the theme of salvation is the poet's presentation of Cain and Abel as opposing characters of good and evil will, and the depiction of Adam and Eve as obedient and repentant subjects of God. The "virtuous" brother, whose selfless love for God is matched only by his faith and his devotion, is analogized with the figure of Christ, thus establishing with Abel's death a *"remedium naturae,"* which absolves the first humans of their offense (16). Adam and Eve's penitent attitude and submission toward God show the Spanish public the proper attitude that will permit the first couple to be among those souls who leave limbo with Christ's harrowing of Hell. In the words of Glaser:

> [t]he vindication of Adam and Eve as well as that of Abel confirms that the play bears on the comprehensiveness of the redemptive work of Christ and not on the universal prevalence of sin and death. In accordance with orthodox teachings Lope shows that even the righteous who lived before the Incarnation will, through the merits of Jesus' Passion, be granted life in heaven, that is to say incorruptibility and immortality. (54-55)

While Glaser has focused on the characters and their actions as a function of the central theme of the play, Julio M. Duarte's study of Lope's Biblical play arrives at a different conclusion: Adam and Eve function to "dramatizar" the Christian concept of Original Sin, and they also "introducen una nota lírica y sentimental" (96). For Duarte,  Adam is affable, "tierno y cariñoso"; however, he possesses a weakness of character that causes him to go astray: "[b]asta que Eva invoque su cariño para que Adán rinda su albedrío" (106). At this point, Lope's portrayal of Adam would appear to be linked to the indulgent Adams of the *Aucto de la prevaricación* . . . and the *Aucto del peccado* . . ., but this similarity is superficial. In Spain's ultra-Catholic environment, any play about Adam must have the predetermined outcome: Adam cannot be portrayed without the notion of his sin; however, each playwright emphasized different aspects of the Genesis B tale, omitting some segments and figures altogether. In Lope's play, his omissions, and his emphasis on the justification for, and the manner in which Adam arrives at his decision to disobey God, make his creation story a novel event.

Lope, like Vélez de Guevara, portrays Adam and Eve in three temporal stages: as young adults, as parents of the adult children Cain and Abel, and finally as grandparents. The most outstanding characteristic of the Adamic personages in Lope's play is their passionate nature, no doubt a reflection of the playwright's dauntless proclivity for love and romance. According to Juan O. Valencia, "[e]l sentimiento íntimo-afectivo lopesco que permea su poesía y teatro es realzado en sus niveles humano y divino en la visión esencialmente afectiva de Adán" (162). It is this aspect of sensuality in Lope's Adam that is most interesting and worthy of further critical attention with regard to the evolution of the figures in Spanish literature.

In representing Adam as the prototype of man, Lope can do nothing less than imitate the models of his society, of his own life, and of his poetic creation; therefore, Lope's Adam becomes the first passionate lover and husband. This is evident in the first words uttered by Adam to Eve, a poetic elaboration on the Biblical verse in Genesis 2:23-24 which presents images of love and union. References to this passage do not appear in the *autos,* and the emotional and vibrant poetics of Lope adds a lyrical dimension to these ideas when he writes these words into his depiction of the character:

> Hermoso pedazo mío,
> Que de mi lado siniestro
> La eterna sabiduría
> Dió materia á su concepto:
> Dulce esposa y compañera,
> Tan igual en los afectos,
> Que sois carne de mis carnes,
> Y siendo mía soy vuestro.
> Fiel esposa y fiel amiga,
> En quien recíproco veo,
> Si no un cuerpo con dos almas,
> Un alma, sí, con dos cuerpos. (179)

Taking the idea of the creation of Eve and the vague notion of marital union presented in the Genesis, Lope injects a sensuality into the relationship of the first humans that is more suggestive of the erotic Song of Songs than any other Biblical notion of love. This last line, with its playful conceit on the idea of the union of bodies and souls, places this Adam within a long tradition of lyric poetry on the theme of love. Earthly love is transferred to the spiritual plane in the union of the souls, resulting in the cancellation of the lovers' separate identities.

This topos of the lovers' union leading to death is more pronounced in one of the most dramatic scenes of the play when Lope portrays the conflictive emotional disposition of Adam in his most tortured moment: namely, when he must choose between God's law and Eve's pleas that he join her in consuming the fruit. After Eve's curiosity and Luzbel's instigation have overcome her spouse's warning not to eat the fruit, Adam sees Eve with it and, fearing the worst, begins a speech which leads up to the fateful denial of God. The passages in italics reveal the motive by which Adam is persuaded to break God's law.

> ADAN
> ¡Oh, mujer engañada!
> ¿Cómo el precepto de tu Dios quebraste?
> ¿Cómo, de ti olvidada,
> De tantos beneficios te olvidaste?
> ¿Cómo ¡ay, contraria suerte!
> Diste paso á mi muerte y á tu muerte?
> EVA
> Turbado, esposo, vienes.
> ¿Qué muerte, qué temor, qué dudas pones?
> Come si amor me tienes;
> No te cieguen temores ni pasiones:
> No acredites antojos:
> *Con lágrimas lo pido de mis ojos.* [6]
> ¡Cómo! ¿Que no te obligo?
> *¿Que no te persüado con mi llanto?*
> O tú eres mi enemigo,
> *O, como dices, no me estimas tanto;*
> *Que si tú me quisieras,*
> *¿De qué comiera yo que no comieras?*
> ADAN
> *¡Oh, fuerza incomprensible*
> *de Amor!* ¡Oh voluntad mal conocida,
> Que sabiendo, infalible,
> Que pierde á Dios, la gracia, el ser, la vida,
> Arrastrado y violento
> Se lleva tras de sí el entendimiento!

EVA

Pruébala, esposo mío.

ADAN

¡Oh, Señor! Si me hubiérades formado
Cautivo el albedrío
Con vuestra voluntad santa ajustado,
¡Con qué amor os sirviera,
Puesto que entonces menos mereciera!
  *En mi propia flaqueza*
*El delincuente hallo, y el delito*
*En mi naturaleza,*
*La ocasión y apetito.*
*¿Qué he de hacer, rodeado*
*Del mismo yo, de mi mujer rogado?*

EVA

  ¿Tan poco, esposo mío, te he obligado?

ADAN

Temo la muerte tuya.

EVA

*Poco amor me has mostrado.*

ADAN

Antes es bien que á amor se le atribuya
El negar tu deseo;
*Mas tuyo soy, y de tu amor trofeo.*
  Bien sé que está mi muerte
En comer esta fruta.

EVA

          Come, acaba.

ADAN

Mas por no entristecerte
Como, aunque sé que peco, y más me agrava
Aquesta ciencia mía;
Pero, *¿qué no podrá tanta porfía?*
  Ya los fieros umbrales
De la espantosa muerte he traspasado,
Del bien inmenso, á males;
De la gracia de Dios, al vil pecado;
Del sol, á la tiniebla obscura y fría;
Pero, *¿qué no podrá tanta porfía?*

> Gusté la acerba muerte,
> Gusté el dolor, la pena, el desconsuelo:
> Perdí la mejor suerte:
> Caí precipitado desde el cielo,
> A eterna esclavonía;
> Pero *¿qué no podrá tanta porfía?* (182)

In this short "temptation" scene between Adam and Eve, the Spanish public was shown for the first time a portrayal of Adam that resembled life. Art imitated nature in this example of a Biblical type that is transformed into a vivid dramatic character. Lope maintains Adam's abstract symbolic value as the instigator of human sin, but his character is modeled on the *amante* known so well to the dramatist, with a depth of passion which is indicative of the manner in which Lope lived and felt his love for women. In this dialogue we find the principal conflict of Adam's will and the substantive motives for the character's actions: he is motivated by the "force" of his love for Eve, by sympathy to Eve's tears, and by her doubts about his affection.

Finally, it is Adam's nature, Lope informs us, for him to choose love for his mate over the law of God. Was sexual union, for Lope, the key to the recondite images of the tree in the Genesis B? These images of love in this dialogue are far from the ideals of courtly love, where the lover's desire is the central motif. Nor do we find another model of love in the Middle Ages, the more erotically centered *Roman de la rose*, where the "sexual motif is . . . enveloped by symbolism and mystery and presented in the guise of saintliness" (Huizinga 114). If the first quotation from the play reminds us of the love of the *dolce stil nuovo*, where the act of loving becomes a supreme form of spiritualization, the temptation of Adam by Eve loses this spiritual quality by its insistence on Adam's instinctual inclination toward remaining with his own kind, with his own "flesh," versus obeying the precept of a God that is virtually absent in the play.

It is noteworthy that Lope's treatment of the Genesis B story is a rupture from the hitherto mythical dimension of the tale, with its supernatural characters and its interaction among the human, animal and spiritual realms. Lope's treatment is more realistic, focusing on the humanity of the first couple and, not surprisingly, the exclusion of God as an anthropomorphic being. While the non-allegorical Adamic *autos* and Vélez de Guevara's play included some form of Dios Padre as a character, the absence of God in Lope's play is a natural expression of the poet's world, where God the creator may be felt as interior emotion (Holy Spirit), but is only manifest in exterior, inanimate signs (Christ on the Cross). Thus, this humanization of Adam is made more fruitful homiletically by the spiritualization of God. The gods of the Book of Genesis, both the anthropomorphic Jahweh, the sententious God of the first creation, and the serpent are ostensibly absent in this play. The only supernatural characters are San Miguel and Luzbel, who establish the topos of the rebellion and fall of the angels. It is the figure of Luzbel, who, in a soliloquy, recounts the formation of Adam and Eve. Without the figure of God, the admonition not to eat the fruit is relayed to Eve by Adam. The condemnation sequence where Adam, Eve, and the serpent are scolded by Jahweh, is omitted by Lope. The task of narrating the creation of the world is given to Adam, who, after meeting his newly-formed mate, delivers a speech to her in which he outlines all of the knowledge that he has of the creation. Thus Lope, in touching upon the tradition of the epic hexamerons, brings the creation story to a human level. Excepting the supernatural characters, San Miguel (a *vox dei*) and Luzbel, God the creator is a spiritualized ideal that reveals itself only by God's voice heard on stage.[7] God's approbation or disapproval of Adam and Eve's actions is manifested principally by the forces of the natural world, as when Adam notes that the animals, the trees, the rocks, and the ground have "risen up" against him (182). In depicting Adam as the historical man, Lope had to obey his own perceptions of life. The physical God is absent, and Adam and Eve are depicted as the lovers, the husbands and wives, the parents and grandparents, modeled on the personages of life.

Speaking of poetry in antiquity, Martin S. Bergmann makes the distinction between the glorification of instinct which he calls "sensuous poetry," and the glorification of the object, which he labels as "love poetry" (78). It is important to point out that Lope's Adam does not place Eve as the object of his desire, rather the un-sanctified desire, the instinct, with an unbridled and fateful (natural) impetus, appears to compel Adam to choose his wife's pleas of complicity over the law of an invisible and absent God. This depiction of Adam as lover was congruent with the notion of love in Lope's theater as a whole. Francisco Ruiz Ramón has singled out Lope as the one dramatist whose theater encompasses the gamut of "[t]oda la mitología del amor humano," from divine love to Neoplatonic love to the most extreme carnal love (288). Lope could not be non-religious; he had entered the priesthood in 1614, some four years before the writing of his *La creación del mundo y primera culpa de nuestro padre Adán*. This play, then, may be considered as one of the artifacts of the mature artist's concentration on the spiritual aspects of life. Nevertheless, given the vivacity and spontaneity with which this most prolific of dramatists lived his life and his loves within and without his literary production, it is only fitting that his portrayal of Adam and Eve as sinners be mitigated by his recognition of humanity's natural impulse toward the "sins" of the flesh. The poet-lover, from the beginning of the written word, has expressed his/her willingness to accept future death in order to unite with the beloved. Similarly, Ruiz Ramón has found this tendency in the lover-protagonist in Lope's theater:

> En las comedias de Lope y sus seguidores asistimos, conducidos por los caminos más diversos, al triunfo del amor, que vence todos los obstáculos, salta todas las barreras, burla todas las normas, invalida todas las reglas, libera todas las potencias del ser humano— inteligencia, voluntad, instinto, ingenio, fantasía—, exalta la totalidad del vivir personal. . . El protagonista de la *comedia del amor* no es ni la mujer ni el hombre, sino la pareja en busca de su mítica unidad original. . . La comedia del amor española es la más prodigiosa recreación del paraíso perdido, que no está más acá o más allá del hombre y su mundo, sino justo donde el amor lo inventa: en el reino de la poesía dramática. (288-289)

Lope's first man, commanded by history and by the political necessities of the church, has to sin. Nevertheless, in forsaking God's paradise, Lope's Adam regained a human paradise in his other self through the instinctual love for his own kind.

In contrast to Luís Vélez de Guevara y Dueñas who depicts Adam as the servant of God, and as a passive figure in the creation scenes, Lope's creation scene focuses on Adam's instinct for love as the motivation for the first sin and on the emotional conflict that Adam suffers before violating God's law. Whereas Lope introduced the formation of the first humans in a speech by Luzbel and omitted the Genesis segments where Adam interacts with God, thus skirting the issue of representing the Almighty on stage, Guevara's inclusion of Dios Padre is more along the lines of the Genesis narrative with its human-like Jahweh. The absence of God in Lope's *La creación del mundo*, serves to accentuate the human element in the play and, consequently, lends a realistic dimension to the work that points to the characterization of Adam and Eve as historical personages rather than types, abstractions, or symbols. Given the sketchy manner in which Vélez de Guevara portrayed Adam, the symbolic value of Original Sin would appear to be this playwright's central message in his creation play, a theme which was most viable for this period in history. While Lope de Vega would portray sin as a necessary characterization of Adam, his justification for the sin, his portrayal of the first man as a lover following heartfelt instincts, and the omission of the castigating God all serve to mitigate the severity of Adam's breach.

In the *auto sacramental*, as in most didactic modes of expression, the lines that separate the theological message and art become rather ill-defined. However, if we can speculate about the possibility of a religious aesthetics, the Adamic *autos* and the Adamic plays make superb touchstones for investigating the marriage of religious myth and theological symbol to the precepts of drama in early modern Spain. In this chapter I have attempted to show the importance of Adam and his "sin" within the religious climate of this period, where at the peak of its cultural significance, the Adamic *autos* and the dramas became necessary media for the propagation of the precepts of the Church, and where the notion of Original Sin served as a defense against the Protestant schism. In the *autos* and in *La creación del mundo* by Vélez de Guevara, the depiction of Adam is subordinate to the figure's function as theological symbol, pointing out humanity's sin and Christ's redemption. Although Lope de Vega utilized the same Biblical and theological models, his skill and creativity as a dramatist and his tendency to make art which was patterned on his own life precluded him from representing Adam as a mere figure. In light of Lope's portrayal of a passionate Adam, we may say that dogmatism of Spanish theology had been compromised by the pen of a truly humanistic artist.

# Chapter Three:

## The Aesthetics of *Paradise Lost* and the Defense of Creation

In 1777 Gaspar Melchor de Jovellanos began translating the first canto of Milton's *Paradise Lost*, dedicating some twenty years to the task without even attempting the remaining eleven cantos. From 1785 to 1799, *Paradise Lost* was the model and inspiration for four lengthy narrative poems in Spanish by some of the country's leading men of letters. Juan Meléndez Valdés composed his "La caída de Luzbel" around 1784 in response to a literary contest held by the Spanish Academy in Madrid the following year. A poem of the same title, possibly submitted for the same contest, was published in Palencia in 1786 by Manuel Pérez Valderrábano. Fourteen years later, in 1799, two of the founding members of the *Academia de Letras Humanas* de Sevilla, Alberto Lista and Félix José Reinoso, each composed poems entitled "La inocencia perdida" that were the culmination of a competition held by that Academy in which a heroic poem on the theme of the Fall was required. Meléndez Valdés, Pérez Valderrábano, Lista and Reinoso were each a part of Spanish "discovery" of *Paradise Lost*, a work which would continue to be translated in verse and prose in the nineteenth century. The relationship between Milton's poem and the Spanish poets of the nineteenth-century who composed adaptations of the myth of the Fall of Man and the vitality of the myth in this period raises the question of artistic influence.

The importance of *Paradise Lost* and its relationship to the poems that followed it may be summarized by Harold Bloom's statement that Milton is the "central problem in any theory and history of poetic influence in English" (*The Anxiety of Influence* 33). Is it true that a great writer looms like an imposing *bête noir* over his successors' efforts? Do the texts left by a great poet constitute the axis of the successors' creative problems? In his analysis of Milton's effects on subsequent poets, Bloom labels the Enlightenment in England the "Milton-haunted eighteenth century" in which the term "haunted" emphasizes the creative spirit of the master poet that inhibits the newcomer, stifling his expression and leaving him with pangs of artistic inadequacy. For Bloom, Milton is the "great Inhibitor, the Sphinx who strangles even strong imaginations in their cradles" (32). Bloom's opinion of Milton is not universal, however. Dustin Griffin contests Bloom's notion of literary oppression of post-Renaissance English

writers in the article, "Milton's Literary Influence." Again referring to the Enlightenment in England, Griffin writes that there are two general misconceptions
about Milton's affect: the first concerns the creation of a "dreary Miltonism of
blank verse poets" who have been influenced negatively by Milton; and the
second involves the idea that the epic genre was made impossible for succeeding
generations by the creation of the greatest epic in the English language (245).
Bloom's argument misrepresents the literary world, writes Griffin, who believes
that Milton's influence in England in effect promoted the writing of epic, because the heroic genre was considered prestigious at the time and its conven-
tions were known and discussed by great poets such as Dryden and Pope (247-
248). While the exact nature of Milton's influence among the English poets is
disputable, it is certain that Milton's poem presented both a problem and a challenge for all writers who succeeded him, including the Spanish.

The English language was a significant factor affecting the reception of
*Paradise Lost* in Spain. E. Allison Peers, who has studied Milton in Spain,
writes that Milton's influence on Spanish literature was essentially insignificant.
Despite the fact that Milton was recognized as being the poet of a great work,
and that translations were made of *Paradise Lost*, he was "appreciated, commented upon and criticized by one after another of the greatest authors of the
day;" yet, according to Peers, neither Milton nor his poetry has exerted significant influence on Spanish letters because the English poet was so unlike the
Spanish in character and genius (169). While Peers finds no affinities between
Milton and the Spanish, considering the poetry contests by the academies and
the translations of Milton's poem it is clear that Milton and his Spanish admirers
shared at least some aesthetic concerns. This particular relationship between
precursor and successor poets merits further investigation.

The story of Milton in Spain is essentially the story of *Paradise Lost*; for,
more than the poet, the text was the focus of interest and a problem for the
Spaniards among whom the poem had become known. The translation into
Spanish of the English epic was not immediate, and the poem became known to
the Spanish in a piecemeal fashion due to the fact that the English language was
not part of the Spanish Academy. Nigel Glendinning, in his study of the relationship between English literature and the Spanish eighteenth century, notes
that in spite of the fact that there was a reasonable amount of foreign exchange
between Spain and England at this time, there seems to have been little opportu-
nity for the Spanish to study the English language (53). It seems that English
literary works were not allowed into the country due to the nature of the Church
in the eighteenth century, and there was little demand for English literature since

so few people knew English (Glendinning 69). At the beginning of the second half of the century, Cadalso, who had perfected his English in trips to Great Britain, states in a letter to Father Diego Lozano that the language of Shakespeare was not popular in Spain. Even at the end of the century, English was not given any priority in Peninsular education. Jovellanos apparently learned the language by means of a grammar book, dictionaries, and perhaps the occasional help of an English traveler, and he later instituted a professorship of English in the Royal Asturian Institute (Glendinning 65-68). While it is uncertain who is responsible for making Milton known in Spain, one of the principal *tertulias* that accounted for the diffusion of the English language and its literature was the Olavide group in Seville, where, it is reported, Jovellanos learned English; thus, it was in Seville that his interest in Milton most likely began (Peers 170). From Seville, Jovellanos no doubt shared his interest with his colleagues in Madrid (Glendinning 91). Word of *Paradise Lost* spread among the literary societies, and by the end of the century, Milton's epic had commanded the attention of many of Spain's most important men of letters. Spain discovered *Paradise Lost* over a century after it had been written and found it a challenging literary model for the age. The timing of the first translations, the subject matter of Milton's poem, and the ruling Neoclassical aesthetic that existed during the latter half of the eighteenth century in Spain contributed to the first Spanish epic cantos about the myth of the fall of Man.

Ignacio de Luzán was one of the first to translate fragments of Milton's poem. Peers notes that Arteaga emended his *Poética* of 1737 with the mention of Milton and a few brief prose translations of his epic. In 1754 the *Orígenes de la poesía castellana* by Velázquez recounts that Alonso Dalda was completing the only known translation of the poem at that time. Estéban de Arteaga refers to a translation by Antonio Palazuelos in 1778, but it is not certain if this was completed and circulated or published. Jovellanos began translating the first canto in unrhymed hendecasyllable verses around 1777, and Meléndez Valdés was asked to comment and edit the translation (170-74). The result of Jovellanos's translation, according to William E. Colford, were Meléndez Valdés's poem "La caída de Luzbel," which is a "close imitation of portions" of *Paradise Lost* written in rhymed octaves that fail to reach the "loftiness" of Milton. Colford explains that "La caída de Luzbel" was written at a time that coincided with a contest held by the Spanish Academy in 1785 for a poem on that subject consisting of less than 100 octave stanzas. A poem of the same title was written by Manuel Pérez Valderrábano (Palencia, 1786) yet there is no evidence of a prize being awarded to either man (201). Milton influenced Meléndez to the point of direct imitation, but it had been Jovellano's idea to attempt the poem on the fall of Luzbel when he challenged his colleagues in his poem "Jovino a sus amigos de Salamanca" that each should compose a certain style of poetry: Diego González was urged to write about religion and philosophy, Liseño (P. Fernández) was to write dramatic pieces on "virtuous subjects" and Batilo (Meléndez) was given the task of writing heroic verse to glorify Spain's past (Colford 202). It was obvious that Meléndez' strength was the lyric, and the poet himself must have been somewhat dissatisfied with his poem, writes Colford, for he never again attempted an epic (202). Since Milton began his poem with the myth of the Fall of the rebel angels, Meléndez' imitation deals with this myth alone and does not treat either of the creation stories. I mentioned this poem only for its having been inspired by Jovellanos' translation of Milton's first canto and to point out the general interest for *Paradise Lost* on the part of the Real Academia Española in the latter part of the eighteenth century.[1]

Why did the Spanish translate Milton's poem? According to Glendinning, the answer lies in the progressive tendencies of the Enlightenment. The ideological tenor, at least among a significant number of intellectuals, was one of openness, of moving beyond national borders in order to find knowledge that might contribute to the progress of society and culture. It was the supra-national, cosmopolitan nature of the men of the Enlightenment that motivated them to explore art from foreign lands, not because their national literary environment was in any way insufficient in inspiration; rather, they were prone to accept anything that might be beneficial no matter what its origin (53). Jovellanos' translation is described by José Benito A. Buylla as "sonora y bien construida versificación" with "estricta y escrupulosa fidelidad al original" (1). As to the question of why Jovino translated the poem, Buylla believes that the spirit of the age and the character of each poet led Jovellanos to translate Milton, who was already a universal figure and his epic a renowned work: "el neoclasicismo de Jovellanos y su época se convenía bien con el clasicismo miltoniano, y la misma forma poética miltoniana —versos largos, períodos más largos aún, cierto hipérbaton— se correspondía claramente con la forma predilecta de Jovino" (2). Buylla describes an affinity between Jovino and Milton as a sort of shared cerebral passion: "un entusiasmo de la razón" that held the unbridled instinct as despicable (2-3).

The genre, the religious theme, the classicist adherence to the precepts and to literary models all contributed to the appeal of *Paradise Lost* in Spain. Writes Glendinning, "[l]as imitaciones o los ecos de la literatura inglesa en la literatura española de fines del siglo XVIII demuestran el interés que se tenía por determinadas ideas y estilos o géneros determinados," (53-54). Nevertheless, the Spanish were discriminating in what they adopted from abroad, choosing what seemed useful and rejecting the rest (Glendinning 91-92). Jovellanos did not translate the remaining eleven cantos of *Paradise Lost* perhaps because of the difficulty he encountered with the first, but Alberto Lista and José Félix Reinoso created original poems modeled on Milton's theme, genre and style, albeit considerably less accomplished than the English poet's epic. A brief overview of the *Academia de Letras Humanas de Sevilla* can offer insight into the poets, their aesthetic ideals, and the poems that resulted from the contest on the theme of lost innocence.

The *Academia Particular de Letras Humanas* was created by Reinoso and José María Roldán in 1793, and it was founded on religious and aesthetic ideals. The meetings were frequented by theologians who had a special interest in Hispanic letters. Reinoso formed the Academy during the beginning of his academic years, a time marked by much poetic activity and a concentrated study of national and classical models. According to Antonio Rafael Ríos Santos, who has studied the *actas* and the histories of the Academy, Reinoso was the most important figure, the "clave que lanzó y sostuvo a esta institución" however, Reinoso must be considered as a component of the group that influenced him: Manuel María de Arjona, Lista, Blanco, José María Roldán, Francisco Núñez y Díaz, García Mora, Justino Matute and Manuel María del Mármol are the members that form a generational group since all were born around 1772, the year of Reinoso's birth (406). The motivation behind the formation of the Academy was in keeping with the age of reformation, for the members believed that Spain had been suffering from a cultural disintegration that had not been sufficiently addressed by other academies. Lista's biographer, Hans Juretschke, writing about the formation of the Academy, states that

> [s]u acto había surgido del deseo de formarse, pero no menos fuerte había sido la voluntad de manifestar su discrepancia con el ambiente. Creían que la cultura patria estaba en decadencia, y su propósito era de regeneración en la poesía y en el saber por medio de la Humanidades, ya que a su parecer, el fomento oficial por academias y certámenes había surtido escasísimo efecto. (19-20)

Sharing a common disdain for the contemporary state of Spanish poetry which according to the Academy was marked by a prosaic and popular *coplerismo* in an exaggerated culteranista style, the members of the Seville school dedicated much energy to creative and critical activities that would serve to remedy the current degenerate state of Spanish letters.

The contests were for the purpose of making the meetings more alluring and were of local interest only, but the second major contest dedicated to the theme of the Fall gained the attention of poets from Madrid. The theme, the form and the relative length had been determined by the group. The rules stated that lost innocence was to be the theme; and that the poem should consist of a canto of around eighty octaves describing the Fall of the first parents (Juretschke 25). The relationship between Reinoso, Lista and Blanco no doubt fomented the interest in and the comprehension of *Paradise Lost* among the Seville poets, for Blanco more than any other Spaniard was fluent in English and could appreciate the complexities of Milton's poem. Nevertheless, the task would prove to be an especially challenging one for the participants. Ríos Santos writes that the theme was proposed on the 8th of December of 1796, and that by May of 1797 not one poet had completed the task. After the allotted period of time the participants suggested that the length be expanded, because the theme required a longer form, and also because of "el grandioso modelo que suponía la obra de Milton sobre aquel asunto, que en el poeta inglés tiene además una amplitud incomparable" (242). Not only was the breadth of the subject problematic for the poets, the contest drew the attention of the capital when the group's selected judge, Juan Pablo Forner, died, necessitating a replacement. Meléndez was chosen and he accepted reluctantly (because, he thought, the Seville poets were unknowns), but he also was unable to fufill the task as judge, due to his untimely exile. Finally the members of the Academy themselves decided to judge the poems, and Reinoso was given the honor for best work (Juretschke 25).

Díaz-Plaja has expressed that of the Spanish academies the Seville school is singular due to its adherence to the aesthetic ideals of the Renaissance; the *Academia de Letras Humanas* is of interest, because the group represents the "último brote de poesía española informada por las doctrinas literarias del Renacimiento" (280). The Seville school's continuation of Renaissance aesthetics is notable principally in its adherence to the systematized rules of the classical age, in its preference for certain genres and, finally, in its continuation of the pervasive religious spirit of that dynamic age. From an aesthetic point of view, the choice of Milton's form and theme was ideally suited to the Academy. The outlook of the members of the Seville school was chiefly neoclassicist and rationalist, and their aesthetics were not divorced from ethical considerations. At a time in which classicism dominated all the literary arts, the members of the

Seville school devoted much attention to classical models because of the belief that good art was based on imitation.

The eighteenth century in Spain is not a period of creation, as Juan Luis Alborg reminds us; rather, of inquiry, examination, and systemization. Its models were classical antiquity and the great writers of the Renaissance (14-16). The overall goal of the Academy was the propagation of "el buen gusto y los verdaderos principios literarios," but it was generally held that the precepts and the necessary "buen gusto" were useless without the gift of "genio" (Lasso 37-38). At the meetings of the *Academia de Letras Humanas*, poetry and oratory were discussed at length along with the classical texts and the authors of the Golden Age. Members of the Seville school were influenced by Herrera and Garcilaso. Lista's Spanish model was Rioja, but above all, Horace from whom Lista inherited the recipe for the ideal literary artist: an inseparable mixture of talent and instruction (Juretschke 270). The precepts of Luzán and the poems of Meléndez were often the topics of conversation and study, and Meléndez, recognized as the most talented contemporary, was considered by Lista and the Seville group as the poet most capable of reviving peninsular poetry, which had become exhausted by an excessive imitation of Góngora's pedantic style (Lasso 71).

While the classical authors and the poetic precepts guided literary composition, the Christian era was the inspiration for many of the group's themes. Valbuena Prat, in *El sentido católico en la literatura española*, characterizes the Spanish eighteenth century as one which derives its essence from religious and Catholic values. Even the most heterodox of authors, he notes, wrote their best works "en tono e inspiración netamente cristianos" (147). This was especially true for the Seville school, and since all of the members of the Academy were theologians, it is not surprising that there was a special fondness for religious poetry. All the members wrote sacred verse and were concerned with the integration of Christian themes into literature. Ríos Santos attributes Reinoso's fondness for religious themes to his profound religious sentiment, which was derived in part from the atmosphere of the Academy (408). He describes the poet as an "intelectual basado en arraigados principios cristianos. El mundo clerical en el que entró en plena juventud, y el espíritu devoto que se ve en los estatutos de la *Academia de Letras Humanas*, explican que su poesía tenga en gran proporción una temática religiosa" (309).

For Lista, literature was necessary for the moral development of society, but it was secondary to the ideas which are shaped by each era and each society. Donald E. Schurlknight describes Lista's view of Christianity and literature as being influenced by Schlegel's notion of "historic" Romanticism as opposed to "liberal" Romanticism. Schlegel's philosophy is based on Christianity as a dividing point between the classical era and the modern or romantic era. For Lista, the adjective *romantic* had to do with "lo perteneciente a la literatura cristiana y monárquica, propia de nuestra civilización actual" (169). Thus Lista could speak of a Romanticism of the sixteenth and seventeenth centuries as being a reflection of the ideal union of ideas and art. Liberal Romanticism was objectionable to Lista on aesthetic and ethical grounds. In his essay on the modern Seville school of literature, Lista railed against the "anarquía intelectual de la época [que] desconoce toda regla y desprecia toda imitación" (257). For Lista, the aim of art is to please, however, it can only do so if constructed according to the rules. As a classicist, Lista held that there could be no poetry without the tested precepts of antiquity and imitation of the masters, but above all, literature should have a moral function: it could produce moral effects and it should "halagar la fantasía con la descripción de la belleza, y debe elegir en el campo moral lo bello y no lo deforme" (Schurlknight 176). On the other hand, the purpose of "liberal" Romanticism was to destroy order in society for the purpose of establishing immorality. Liberal Romanticism was destructive of society because it dared to present bad examples of conduct regarding morals, religion and politics (Schurlknight 175).

The popularity of *Paradise Lost* also demonstrated an interest in the epic as a genre. In his essays Lista examined the precepts of the ancients to determine if these were applicable to the literature of his own day. The restoration of classical genres was one of his goals, and he praised the "advantages" of the descriptive poem and he created a perceptive guideline for its composition. He believed that mythological images and the pastoral convention were "suitable" for the modern composition and that narrative poetry and especially epic poetry fit the "spirit of the time" (Metford 27-28). In his article on the epic genre in the seventeenth and eighteenth centuries, Frank Pierce notes that the epic was attractive to the neoclassicists because they were in many ways the poetic brothers of Milton, not the least of which was their desire to produce that "most august medium" of all. The *canto épico*, a short narrative poem in cantos, played an important part in eighteenth-century letters, because

[i]t became a heroic form well adapted to the feelings of the age, while at the same time its origin, form and tradition gave it a particular charm for the academies. What more lofty genre in which an aspiring poet might declaim his skill and impress his fellow-members? (15)

The religious epic had been popular in the seventeenth century and it remained fashionable throughout the eighteenth century. Given the inclination of the Seville poets towards classical forms and the Renaissance poets, it is understandable that *Paradise Lost* would be well received among this group, which traditionally cultivated the theological and Biblical themes contained in Milton's epic.

Commenting on the theme and the form of Milton's poem, Pierce notes: "[i]t is not a singular fact that *Paradise Lost* should appeal to a nation that had long indulged its love of the *poema sacro* and of the eschatological, and had produced not a few outstanding poems on related themes" (32). Most certainly the religious theme, the heroic genre, and the aesthetic ideal of the age were the common bonds that linked the Spanish poets to the English bard. The late appearance of *Paradise Lost* in Spain coincided with a continuation of the epic genre and religious themes of the Renaissance among the neoclassicists. Milton, contrary to the opinion of Peers, was indeed the classical and spiritual "brother" of the Spaniards and their attention to the classical precepts and the affirmation of the ideal of art serving the ethical and moral truths of Christianity made Milton's version of the Fall of man a timely and ambitious model. Perhaps these elements were more important factors in the popularity of *Paradise Lost* in Spain than was the text itself, given that the poem arrived piecemeal and that it took more than a century to achieve a translation of the entire text into Spanish.

Nevertheless, the theme, the form, and the limited time frame were obviously too ambitious for all but the most talented of poets. Reinoso and Lista accepted a formidable challenge when they attempted to equal Milton. In the introduction to his edition of *Paradise Lost*, Merritt Y. Hughes has called the theme of the creation "the great epic theme" of the seventeenth century. For Milton and his contemporaries, the story of Adam and Eve represented a theory of history and an optimistic promise of paradise regained in its "redemptive hope for both humanity in general and for individual men" (xvi). Originally inspired by the Christian drama with its roots in the medieval mystery plays, Milton was influenced as well by a contemporary resurgence of the Genesis tradition in Holland and Italy. While still a child, the future poet had read the *Divine Weeks* by Sieur du Bartas as well as Tasso's *Il mondo creato*. As an adult he came to know Grotius' *Adamus Exul* and Giambattista Andreini's *L'Adamo*. *Paradise Lost* had been originally conceived as a drama, though in contrast to the mystery plays, Milton did not limit his work to the Christian tradition. Classical authors provided much material for his dramatic poem, especially in regard to the myth of the fall of the angels and the character of Satan. In his rendition of the Fall story, Milton achieved the imaginative and densely allusive literary culmination of the dramatic and poetic recreations of the Celestial Cycle: the dramatic presentation of the Fall of the rebel angels, the Creation and Fall of man, and the Announcement of the coming of the Redeemer. Milton had attained the grandeur of his classical predecessors, and he surpassed them in his complex amalgamation of tone and genre that was recognized in his own time as characteristic of a truly great work of art.

Why did Milton choose to write the story in epic form when a tragedy would have been a logical choice? Marianna Woodhull has written that since Milton's Adamic tale is an extension of the conflict between the rebel angels and God, the narrative material was too extensive for the limiting structure of a tragedy; the story requires the "whole background of the infinite" (15). A second reason for the epic genre is the fact that the incidents included belong to the fantastic or marvelous, and the narrator's voice in the poem is preferable to the actor's narration of cosmic passages and events. Finally, given the fact that Milton's religious beliefs would compel him to place Christ as the dominant force over Satan, Man's fall is not to be perceived as a tragedy for humanity; but rather, *Paradise Lost* is a Christian epic, showing Christ as the hero who will lead humanity to a triumphant reunion with God (15-16).

Under the influence of *Paradise Lost* and the epic genre, the Genesis creation stories were amended with a new beginning. Milton's achievement had sanctified the primitive combat myth by making it a major part of the Christian history of salvation. Milton's inclusion of the story of the Adversary, God's first enemy, into the Genesis myths legitimized the figure of Satan, the realm of the underworld, and the Devil's role as the "true" source of evil in the world. Furthermore, Christian "history" was expanded, opening up a time before the Biblical Genesis. In this manner, Milton's epic is responsible for stimulating the interest of the West in the subject of the nefarious, the darker realm, and its characteristic evil.

This brings us back to the idea of myth, for in the view of Neil Forsyth, Satan is the figure that gives the Christian religion its mythological dimension:

> The depredations and tyranny of Satan are what motivate the incarnation story and that against which the activities of Christ are directed. The myth is most evident in those parts of the Christian testament which are explicitly apocalyptic, but it is present wherever the Satan figure or his demonic allies appear. (8)

The priestly editors of the Adamic myth had erased practically all traces of Satan in the Genesis A text. Milton's treatment of the monstrous winged figure resting on the fiery water reminds us of the ancient Levant myth. Milton gave us a modern reenactment of the pre-creation time, when the shining Marduk, the powerful young hero, battles the fearsome Tiamat, the dark dragon out of whose split carcass the matter of the universe is formed. Here is the eternal, human desire for order over chaos that would become the Genesis A creation of the world from the Biblical "darkness over the face of the abyss," the only uncensored remnants of the tale of the satanic dragon. The order-out-of-chaos motif is the heart of the myth of the Adversary. Rather than blame Eve, the talking serpent, or Adam, the myth of Satan centers the origin of evil on its primeval source: God's "old enemy," the angel that had dared to be equal to the Creator. Since Milton's epic entailed the representation of Christ as the hero, the characters of God and the Son would require creative episodes that would utilize and modify the two treatments of the Supreme Being which had been presented in Genesis A and B.

Jovellanos, Meléndez Valdés, Valderrábano, Arenzana, Lista and Reinoso were very interested in Milton's work for what Milton had done to the figure of Satan. Mario Praz, describing the metamorphosis of Satan in literature, remarks that never had anyone conferred upon the enemy of God such an "aspect of fallen beauty, of splendour shadowed by sadness and death" (59). Bloom is one contemporary critic that considers Satan the true hero of *Paradise Lost*, calling the figure the major personality of the epic, to the extent that not even Christian nor Hebrew writers contributed so greatly to the ancient combat myth. In comparison, one of the paradoxes of the poem is that Christ is an aesthetic and spiritual "disaster," due to Milton's placing him in a chariot, "leading an armored attack upon the hapless hoplites of Satan's legions" (*Ruin* 105-106). In the latter part of the eighteenth century, the "sinister charm" of Milton's Satan would fuse with the type of the sublime criminal, and the Romantics would become fascinated with the combination of the sinister, the rebel, and the sublime (Praz 59).

### Lista's *La inocencia perdida*

A close reading of Lista's and Reinoso's poems shows that the Seville group did not utilize Milton's entire poem as a model; but rather, only selected parts of the work guided their writing. Speaking of the motive for the Adamic theme and the model of the poems, Peers comments on the poems' major flaw:

> Probably the extent to which notable Spanish writers had been influenced by Milton was the reason which underlay the proposal by the *Academia de Letras Humanas* of a subject for its competition so evidently inspired by him. Neither Reinoso nor Lista had Milton's gifts, Milton's temperament or Milton's opportunities. They nevertheless produced laudable enough poems . . . . The fact that the dimensions of "La inocencia perdida" were necessarily much smaller that *Paradise Lost* was against [the poem], even had Reinoso been a second Milton. (176)

The length is the most notable difference between the Spanish poems and the English epic. Milton composed his first canto of 798 verses and the average length for each of his twelve cantos was 880 verses. Lista recounted the entire Celestial Cycle in 720 verses and Reinoso extended the tale to 1,136 verses. Understandably, the development of the characters and incidents in the Spanish versions was much more limited than in Milton's poem. In addition, the narrative structure of the Spanish poems, the order in which the incidents take place, does not follow Milton's poem except in the most general sense. All the poems open with an invocation, then proceed to develop a scene of the fallen Satan and the angels in the abyss, who somehow receive knowledge of the creation of man. The Spanish poets then move to a description of Eden and the creation of Eve, while Milton develops the notion of God's foreknowledge of the Fall, and the Son offers himself as redemption. To Milton, and thus, to Protestantism generally, the idea that God was all powerful and omniscient meant that the rebellion of Lucifer, the temptation of Adam and Eve, and the expulsion from Eden were an elaborate plan that God had devised in order to offer humans the possibility of salvation. This is a major difference between *Paradise Lost* and the Seville poems which treat Luzbel as a true rebel. The only other major points of contact between Milton and the Seville poets is the episode of the temptation of Eve by the serpent, and the ending of the poems with the expulsion of Adam and Eve from Eden.

Lista's poem reduces the figures of Adam and Eve to minimal character types of few actions and no speech. The humans are nondescript pawns in the greater cosmic conflict between Satan and God. Contrary to the dramatic Adamic works, Lista's Adam and Eve do not speak, their actions are narrated, and they are simply acted upon. Satan, God, and the poet are the only prominent voices in the narration. Nevertheless, Lista fails to develop these characters beyond the simple type. Neither do the figures of God, Christ, or Satan achieve any heroic dimension in the poem. The chief focus of the Spanish poems is the battle between Heaven and Hell, and the plotting of the rebel angels to continue the war against God by attacking the humans. Lista presents the fallen Satan at rest on the fiery lake where his accomplices are assembled around him. Seeing that God has created man, the Adversary burns with envy and anger; and he considers the new creation as a challenge to the Almighty. Deliberating on the nature of God's omnipotence and the impossibility of battling directly with God, Luzbel conceives that it is possible to assail God by deceiving the new being and perverting his gift of free will. Satan then sends Soberbia and Astucia to Eden to spoil the creation by causing man to break God's precept. Since pride is the first sin of this angel, the "rebelde Querube" expresses a dauntless pride in his defeated and fallen state that is reminiscent of Milton's Satan, though this Spanish Satan does not approach the heroic stature of the Adversary of *Paradise Lost*. One place where Lista's Satan approximates Milton is when the rebel angel exhibits a healthy acceptance of his fallen condition:

> Una salud nos da nuestra rüína,
> Y es no esperar salud, si ya vencido
> El despiadado cielo me destina
> A eterna rabia e inmortal gemido;
> ¿Qué temeré de la aversión divina?
> Cuando con nuevas iras despedido
> Vibre de su justicia el rayo fuerte
> ¿Podrá ser mas acerba nuestra suerte? (17)

Lista then begins his description of Eden, and his garden paradise is a bountiful and harmonious place created for the glory of the Almighty: "Y todo el universo en mudo canto / Entona a su Criador el himno santo / . . . / Para figura de su gloria quiso / Formar de Eden el bello paraíso" (28-29). Lista does not develop to any notable extent the characters of the humans. The decisive moment when Eve decides to eat the fruit is given slight dramatic effect:

> La primera madre por sus venas siente
> Crecer no resistida la impía llama,
> Y la ambición del mando onmipotente

> Y el esplendor de eterna luz la inflama;
> Del devorante ardor ciega la mente
> La mano tiende a la funesta rama;
> Tres veces en troncar su fruto insiste,
> Y tres la poma indócil le resiste. (54)

The temptation of Adam, like the Genesis model, is nondescript, for he acquiesces without words of protest.

Lista's God is essentially a reincarnation of the childlike Jahweh in his unpredictable temperament, but in an attempt to capture the epic tone, Lista gives his God a thundering voice. After God learns of the transgression, the heavens open up with red lights, thunder and lightning crash, and thousands of angels appear: "Rasgado el cielo en hórrido estallido; / Tembló el eje inmortal; el polo truena / Y el ancho mundo gime sacudido; /Roja luz el inmenso espacio llena / En coladores rayos encendido; / Bañado en fuego el aire resplandece, / Y el trono del Altísimo aparece" (66). Luzbel tries to flee but "fierce" angels detain him. God speaks, expressing his wrath, inculpating the humans and commanding the earth and its creatures to avenge the transgression. The Genesis verse where Jahweh walks in search of the couple is given a thunderous roar, showing God jealous of the threat to his power:

> Y ¿Dó están? dice: ¿La caterva impía
> Burlará mi poder, o a mi ira armada
> Se librará? ¿Dó están? ¿La tiranía
> Alzará contra mí su frente osada?
> En cielo y tierra la potencia es mía;
> Yo el Señor de las huestes; hacinada
> Está, cual heno vil la grey traidora,
> Y el ardor de mi aliento los devora. (69)

Lista has his Almighty condemn the serpent, ignoring Luzbel who is being held by the angels. Suddenly this God of vengeance without pardon becomes the God of mercy, and He commands the Son to be the victim of his justice. God tells how his Son's death will redeem the creation and that he will return to judge all the nations:

> Tú, de mi inmenso ser inmensa lumbre,
> Hijo querido de eternal delicia,

> Tú, vistiendo la ajena servidumbre,
> La víctima serás de mi justicia.
> Verás el rostro, humana muchedumbre,
> Dispuesto el rayo a mi piedad propicia,
> Cuando dado al suplicio en alta cima,
> El Rey del cielo moribundo gima. (81)

Neither does Lista attempt to develop the potentially dramatic passages in the Genesis narration. The narration of the creation of Eve moves quickly into the temptation, where the woman, having wandered off alone, is addressed by Astucia in the form of the serpent, who is aided by Soberbia. Whereas in the *autos* much of the dramatic conflict was derived from the scene of temptation between the serpent and Eve, in Lista's poem the serpent entices the woman by praising her beauty and inciting her ambition to be equal to God. Likewise the temptation of Adam, as in the Genesis B version, is immediate and unmodified. Adam eats without question or discourse with Eve. Lista ends his poem with the angels singing in praise of God, the band of rebel angels thrown into the abyss, and Adam, walking away from Eden. Lasso de la Vega expressed uncharacteristic censure of Lista's work noting its lack of energy, movement and vigor. "[H]ay mayor proligidad [sic] en los detalles," notes Lasso, "pero el vuelo de su fantasía es más lento y menos atrevido; aunque no por esto deja de emplear en su obra el tono digno y propio del asunto" (421). Comparing Lista's poem to his aesthetic model leaves much to be desired. Lista believed that art should be a controlled representation based on models, not given to spontaneous effusion, rather directed by the tried precepts of the ancients, and poetry should entail "el ejercicio de una sabia imitación y emulación" (Juretschke 270). Having such a formidable model revealed that the breadth of the material and the form were well beyond his creative abilities. While we should expect that his poem would meet his criteria regarding the role of literature as exemplary of moral behavior, notwithstanding, there is no moral message clearly presented in the text, except perhaps that humans should fear the power of God.

### Reinoso's *La inocencia perdida*

In the opinion of Ríos Santos, the aesthetic principles espoused by the *Academia de Letras Humanas* found their most ardent representative in Reinoso. He was faithful to the Golden Age models and the themes of Classical poetry, being

careful to avoid local color and Andalusian settings, or any hint of popular poetry (282). The same critic describes Reinoso's poetic language as characteristic
of the Seville group in general: a "buscado apartamiento del habla ordinaria, y
retorizante afán renovador" that shows the influence of Herrera (407). Guided
by his theological training and the classical environment of the Academia, Reinoso cultivated religious themes such as virtue, the vices, and evil, and he often
treated these with a classical twist of mythological allusions (408). Reinoso follows Lista in his insistence of poetry as an imitative art (286); and he shared
much of the common poetic fare that Luzán propagated in his *Poética*. *Gusto*
was the sense that distinguished a good imitation from a bad one, again rein-
forcing the notion that the essence of poetry is in imitation of Nature. Beauty
and the Sublime were to be distinguished by objects of inferior or equal status to
man (290).

Reinoso's version of the tale of lost innocence was recognized by the *Academia de Letras Humanas* as the better of the two poems, and is believed to be
Reinoso's most important work, and in the opinion of Ríos Santos, "el mejor en
su género de todo el siglo XVIII español" (407). After the competition Reinoso
polished the poem over a period of several years before publishing it. When the
poem became known to Quintana, he wrote a critique of it in a bimonthly published in Madrid from 1803-1805, the *Variedades de Ciencias, Literatura y Artes*,[2] in which he praised the execution of the poem, but criticized the subject
and the model. The theme did not lend itself to the imagination of the poet, according to Quintana, and the mysteries of the Christian Religion were not material that should be represented as poetic ornaments, a remarkable departure from
the time of the *autos*. Quintana did not think highly of Milton, labeling him 'más
bien que un poeta émulo de Homero, un catedrático que explica lecciones de
teología' (Pierce 33). In his response, the Contestación al juicio sobre el poema
de 'La inocencia perdida', Blanco defended the right of any poet to publish poetry on any theme, religious or not, thus vindicating all the members of the
Seville group (Ríos Santos 312).

The plot of Reinoso's poem may be summarized thus: the sunlight of dawn
assails the angel's eyes as he observes the creation. It is the third day and the
earth is brilliant with colors and light that shimmers on the plants and animals.
As God creates man, all of the animals draw near to admire him. God appears
and all of creation bows down to him: Adam offers songs of praise to the Almighty. The firmament where Luzbel is standing suddenly gives way, and the
angel falls into a lake of "eternal weeping" where he cries out, wondering how
to avenge himself against the new being that will take his place in Heaven.

Luzbel is weak and he considers ceasing the war against God because of his rival's omnipotence. Remembering the prohibition of the fruit, he decides that he will corrupt God's new creature. Having decided that the human will be the objective of the next battle, Luzbel, with new resolve, leaves the lake. Hunger, sickness, old age, vice, impiety and other evils follow behind, reminders of the morality plays that Reinoso had witnessed during the Corpus Christi. The poet ends the first canto by cursing the day when Adam, once lord of the world, fell into shameful bondage.

The second canto begins with the creation of Eve. The poet expresses his inability to describe the love, beauty, and the richness of the original state of innocence. He then presents images that point out the harmony between the first humans and nature. Seeing the tree of knowledge of good and evil, Eve trembles, not daring to draw near. She is curious of its beauty, and suddenly the "horrendous" serpent uncoils. Eve does not flee, for in her innocence she cannot know fear. The serpent explains the prohibition of the fruit and that God fears that the humans will be equal to him if they eat. He explains to her that she and Adam cannot have free will if they are slaves to God. The serpent leaves and Eve vacillates, uncertain and fearful. As she tastes the fruit, she looks up to Heaven and feels a chill in her blood and drops the fruit. Retrieving it she carries it to Adam who immediately eats.

Upon tasting, the universe changes. God sees this and burns with anger. Thunder rolls through the heavens and as God begins to hurl the fiery ray to strike down the humans, the Son stops him, reasoning that pity and love are the best remedies against the human's treacherous act, because their crime was inspired by Luzbel. The Son tells the Father to punish the humans but that He, the Son, will sacrifice himself for their crime. God agrees, responding that in his divine plan he willed this before the creation, and that He and the Son will make an alliance of the world. Here an example of God's precognition as detailed in Milton's poem.

The aesthetic success that Reinoso achieved with his poem is attributable in part to the longer scope of his work. Reinoso develops more complete characters from the mythical types using more speech and dialogues than Lista. Like the poem of his colleague, the figures of Adam and Eve are minor. There is no attempt to develop the relationship between Adam and Eve nor between the humans and God. In fact, Reinoso's humans, like the Adam and Eve of Lista, are mute actors: the poets only narrate their actions which are essentially minimized to the most basic elements of Genesis B, and the description of their pre-lapsarian and post-lapsarian existence in the garden is restricted. As in Lista's poem, Satan, the Almighty, and the Son are the central characters in this cosmic conflict.

Reinoso's poem is closer to its model. Does the poem have a hero? Luzán had written that the epic poem should be characterized by the representation of a great and noble action, by the inclusion of illustrious characters such as kings and heroes; the poem should present some sort of moral instruction, and it should have a believable, entertaining and admirable style (557). Milton had intended to make the Son the heroic figure in his poem but, instead, created a sympathetic character in his Adversary. In Reinoso's poem Satan is described as fierce, a horrendous, flaming monster, whose wrath and enmity against God is expressed in a metaphor of a Mount Etna, trembling with smoke and torrents of flaming rocks spewed upon the valleys, felling forests, fields and oxen, everything in its wake, until finally crashing into the sea (I 13-15).

Not surprisingly, given his Miltonian model, there are also moments in Reinoso's depiction of Satan that touch upon aspects of the sublime criminal that Milton has attributed to the arch fiend. Satan exalts the actions of the rebel angels by characterizing them as heroic. Valor, glory, daring, and heroism are the rewards for subverting the tyranny of Heaven:

> Suya fue, no lo niego, la victoria;
> Mas nuestro es el valor. El yugo odiado
> De servirle rompimos: esta gloria
> No borrará jamás funesto hado.
> Renovarán los siglos la memoria
> De nuestro invicto ardor: de fuego armado,
> Dirán, al Cielo se atrevió el abismo,
> El atreverse solo es heroismo. (1.7)

Although the last line may be interpreted in at least two ways since the use of diacritics had not been regularized at the time of the writing of the poem, I suspect that Reinoso is indicating that the audacity of the act in and of itself is heroic in the eyes of Satan, and that this is somehow sanctioned by the passing of time. At other times, Reinoso's Satan, like his model, is capable of weakness and uncertainty. Satan highlights his sad, tortured condition when he reminds the angels of his deed: "Yo pretendí ser Dios . . . ¡quánto me aflige / Este voraz recuerdo, que acompaño / Con inútil llorar, llorar eterno! / ¡Ay! Ser Dios quise, y arrostré un infierno" (1.41). His sadness is again expressed after he has failed in his first attempt to rise up from the abyss and arrive at Earth to pervert human will. Satan falls back into a lake characterized by its eternal grief. There, weak and weeping, he admits that he is defeated:

> . . . O fiera suerte!
> ¡Necio! clama: ¡quán necio entre destrozos
> Arrastrar pensé al hombre a cruda muerte!
> Solo yo moriré; y en puros gozos
> El lodo inmundo, el lodo ¡pena fuerte!
> La planta ¡o rabia! extenderá atrevido
> sobre el trono a Luzbel solo debido. (1.30)

Then the leader of the rebel band calls for surrender, stating that it is the will of God. This sentiment of defeat is present again briefly when the character contemplates the brilliant radiance of God's presence, vacillates, then resolves not to surrender, showing his determination in the face of insurmountable odds:

> ¡Ay! no, creedme, Dioses, no es posible
> A nuestras fuerzas su eternal ventura
> Trastornar: yo lo he visto. . . ¡Quán terrible
> Se aumenta mi dolor! La lumbre pura,
> La luz que gocé . . . memoria horrible!
> ¡Tiempo, tiempo dichoso! Mas aun dura
> Mi obstinación: el fuego, el fuego ardiente
> Sólo quiero: Luzbel no se arrepiente. (I 34)

Reinoso is able to portray some nuances in the figure of Satan that reminds us of his Miltonian model and the figures of God and the Son exhibit some of the problematic traits that Bloom found in Milton. The character of God is essentially one-dimensional: an all-powerful radiant being that is capable of extreme anger. Reinoso's Almighty fails aesthetically and spiritually in the same way that Milton's Son is a "disaster." God's anger is reflected in nature: when he discovers the transgression, Reinoso describes the sea of fire that burns in his face; the winds and mountains burn, and the clouds become inflamed. Then:

> . . . en la incendida mano
> Presto el rayo nació: la ondosa llama
> En puntos sube, y por el ayre vano,
> Brotando entre los dedos se derrama.

> Iba a lanzarlo ya, y el soberano
> Verbo, alzado en su trono, el Cielo inflama
> De un esplendor de gloria y ambrosía,
> Que amor, su faz bañando, despedía. (2.28)

and in the moment in which Reinoso's "Jahweh" is about to loosen the bolt, the Son responds: "Amor le ofrece ante la diestra alzada" and the God of flaming wrath is convinced by the Son's argument that the death of the humans will mean a victory for his enemy. Reinoso continues the Son's all too human argument: "Padre: la eternal justicia / Debe ser aplacada; no, no pido / Que el rayo pongas sin vengar tu nombre: / ¡Oh! lánzale en tus iras sobre el hombre; (II 32), and the Son then offers himself in sacrifice. Another aesthetic problem in Reinoso's poem has to do with his theme. Like God's anger, the loss of innocence is portrayed by depicting a change in the state of nature. After Adam eats, the sky darkens, the winds become stronger and the animals become wild, converting all the Earth into a "suplicio." Adam and Eve realize their nakedness and it is reported that their former radiance is lost (I 24).

Pierce complimented this poem mentioning how Reinoso's poetic vigor makes his a competent poem: the two works "retain a certain freshness and force in Spanish heroic verse" even though Lista and Reinoso seem to have rendered the subject for its own sake (34-36). There is no doubt that neither Lista nor Reinoso followed their model except in the most general scheme. While they may have wanted to follow Luzán's precepts regarding the epic, creating a lengthy poem that depicted their heroic notions of Christ, on the contrary, their poems failed. Instead, their works pointed out the flaws in the Christian myth: the talking snake, the forbidden fruit, the lost innocence, and the angry Jahweh of the Genesis B creation story at a time when the "mysteries" of Christianity were beginning to fall under the scrutiny of rational eyes. In addition, Reinoso's poem was close to capturing the sympathetic qualities that Milton had imagined, consciously or not, for his figure of Satan. To Lista, Reinoso's poem might be considered Romantic for its theme; but perhaps Reinoso's Satan is indicative of a pre-Romantic trait (in the sense of liberal Romanticism) that coexists within the profound classicism of this member of the Seville school.

Lista believed that the Spaniards had previously failed in the epic because they had "traspasado con demasiada libertad los límites del arte" (Lista 247). Later, he promoted the form by calling for a young poet who could write in this most respectable genre a poem "worthy of Spanish literature" (Metford 27-28). While the dramatists who recreated the Adamic myth were motivated by theological reasons associated with the Counter-Reformation, and while it has been written that Milton's motivation was to rival Moses as the great prophet of Cristianity in his attempt to "justify the ways of God to men" (Hughes 6), it is obvious that the Seville poets were not guided by such ambitious or lofty design. Formal aesthetics were the guiding factor for the Seville poets, for it seems that they were more interested in justifying their own abilities as poets. Holding up as their ultimate model a literary giant who had written a timely and worthy theme in the most honorable of poetic forms reveals much about what Reinoso and Lista had read of Milton's epic. Reading only pieces, or summaries, of the work protected them from the English "Sphinx." Rather than experiencing an "anxiety of influence" due to the existence of the great world of art that represented a culmination of theme, form, and content, the Spanish poets were challenged by bits and pieces of Milton to create for themselves a Spanish epic that might somehow match Milton's achievement, a difficult task that Lista and Reinoso might have realized, had they been able to read a completed translation of *Paradise Lost*. As to the cultural vitality of the Adamic myth at the end of the eighteenth century, Quintana's critique that the mysteries of Christianity should not be the subject of poetry reveals that the Genesis B was now perceived susceptible to the scrutinizing minds of the Spanish *Ilustrados*.

### La caída de Adán

Bloom has written in *The Anxiety of Influence* that "poems rise not so much in response to a present time, . . . but in response to other poems" (99). His words are especially applicable to Meléndez Valdés, Lista and Reinoso, for the Spanish poems on the theme of lost innocence most certainly arose in response to the news of *Paradise Lost*. The nature of the Spaniards' interest in Milton's epic involved a combination of factors related to the timing of the "discovery" of Milton in Spain, the aesthetic interests of the Spanish poets, and the religiosity of the members of the Seville school. The way the Seville poets chose to deal with the Biblical material had more to do with aesthetic ideals and less to do with the theological concepts related to the myth. Were the Spaniards able to recognize Milton's genius, and did he exert any real influence in Spanish literature at all? The results of Peer's investigation into the influence of Milton in Spain would have us believe that Milton's talent was only recognized during the latter part of the eighteenth century and that it was unlikely that Milton could influence Spanish letters, due to the fact that Spain had "so little sympathy with the England of the Commonwealth" (183). The evidence concerning the origen, the circumstances, and the content of Reinoso's "La inocencia perdida" negate Peer's conclusions.

Likewise, when Víctor Rosselló begins his description of Eden in the second canto of his *La caída de Adán*, he invokes the aid and guidance of Murillo, Rafael, Milton, and Dante, which would lead us to believe that the poet was familiar with works by these artists. There were two translations of *Paradise Lost* that appeared after the Reinoso and Lista poems: Benito Ramón de Hermida and Juan de Escoiquiz, minor writers in rival political and literary schools each undertook a translation of *Paradise Lost* that was published in 1814. In 1849 a literal prose translation of the epic is made by Saura Mascaró. After this, reports Peers, the only evidence of Milton's influence is in future translations. Others appeared between 1870 and 1890. In 1868 Dionisio Sanjuán produced a prose translation and Escoíquiz' work was reprinted in 1873 (173-182). By the composition of Rosselló's poem in 1873, there had been several Spanish translations of Milton's epic, and it is most likely that Rosselló would have had access to one of these. Nevertheless, *La caída de Adán*, an obscure poem by an unknown poet, bears minimal relationship to the English epic, and it is evident that Rosselló did not model his poem on *Paradise Lost*. Rosselló was more creative in his manipulation of the elements of the Genesis material than any of his Spanish precursors. Instead of making Satan a major figure in the poem, Rosselló reduces the combat myth to a few strophes that represent a flashback during the episode of the temptation in the ninth canto. All of the action in the poem is developed in Eden and the actors are those of the Genesis B tale: God, Adam, Eve, the Satan/Serpent figure and various angels. Although *La caída de Adán* approached Milton's work in length, (an invocation of 80 quartet strophes followed by fifteen cantos of between 24 and 61 hendecasyllabic quartets in varying rhyme) the processes and motivations of the temptations and the annunciation of the redemption and the depiction of the characters are not drawn from the English poem. Rosselló combines Genesis B material with much imaginative vigor and Romantic effusiveness to produce a unique twist on the Adamic story that ends up forming an indictment of the Adamic myth. In addition, his poem reflects the cultural vitality of the myth at the latter half of the nineteenth century, a time when tyrants, even mythical ones, were hardly in vogue. Following is a summary of Rosselló's poem.

In the invocation the poet states his profound love for God and his disdain for the world, mentioning that he will always praise God, his wonder, power, and glory. Adam is formed and the Heavens are moved to sing God's praise. The poet describes Eden: a high, walled garden with sculpted gold and marble, filled with infinite plants and animals. God instructs the man to the effect that he is lord over all living things, and the warning is given not to eat from the tree. God forms Eve, and the pair are introduced and told to reproduce to fill the world. Then, a second warning is given against breaking God's mandate. Adam and Eve praise God's omnipotence and his creation. The poet describes Eve's beauty and asks the angels to admire her, and in a digression, the poet expresses his own love for God and for the Creation.

Adam and Eve comment on their existence in Paradise, realizing that this state of perfection will be sustained as long as they are obedient and praise God: "Muy grande será, pues, nuestro contento, / Si a Dios, siempre sumisos y leales, / Guardamos su ley santa y mandamiento: / De esta suerte seremos inmortales" (50). Commenting that their spirits are united with God, Adam notes that they should maintain their eternal praise to God for giving them this perfect condition. At this point, Rosselló depicts his first humans as having foreknowledge of Satan even before they are introduced to the serpent. In a statement of solidarity with God, Adam asks Eve: "¿Pudiéramos, rebeldes y blasfemos, / Alzarnos, contra El, retar su saña? / Jamás pecado tal cometeremos; / No cabe, no en los dos, maldad tamaña," and then he replies: "Jamás inclinaremos nuestra frente, / Ante tu ídolo, Satán maldito; / De Dios queremos ser eternamente; / Nuestro amor hacia El es infinito" (54).

In a digression, the poet describes the first humans in Paradise, and alludes to the rebellion of the angels telling of Luzbel's entrance into the garden. Commenting on Eve's transgression, the poet warns her: "Todavía desviar puedes tu paso, / Huir del lazo, que Satán te tiende, / Y a la tierra evitar un tal fracaso; / No olvides que su suerte de ti pende" (72), then he inculpates her, and asks the angels to intercede to prevent her from undertaking her rebellious act: "Salvad, sí, esa flor tan primorosa, / Alegría del mundo y esperanza; / Salvadla pronto, ¡ay! el tiempo acosa, / Y la tormenta sobre ella avanza" (74).

The serpent is described as a horrible monster with an alluring voice, which, carried by the gentle breeze, seems to enthrall Eve. Rosselló's Satan is described with the following:

> Era un monstruo deforme, cuya cola,
> De acerados dardos coronada,
> Debiera haber bastado, por sí sola,
> Para desviar de Eva la mirada.

> Su boca, cual de cueva tenebrosa,
> De peñascos durísimos cubierta,
> Abríase temible y anchurosa;
> Ante ella la luz temblaba incierta.
>
> Sus ojos, cual volcanes, despedían,
> De llamas y de chispas un torrente;
> Ensortijadas víboras ceñían,
> Cual diadema hórrida, su frente. (77-78)

The poet goes on to describe Satan's discourse with his band, which had occurred just before entering the garden to tempt Eve. Satan plots to corrupt the humans, because it is his destiny to do battle with God forever. Unable to let go of the allegorical figures associated with the Adam and Eve myth, Rosselló introduces the monstrous creatures, Sin and Death, to accompany Satan in Hell. An angel of God warns Satan, who has just finished his discourse to his followers, that he return to the abyss since Christ is the king of the world, and he has given his life for humanity. In a statement that breaks the linear narrative time established earlier by the poem, the poet commands Adam and Eve to leave their tombs, and along with all the souls in Limbo, to adore Christ who has erased their sin:

> Pobres Eva y Adán, seres caídos,
> de la tumba salid en este instante,
> Para adorar sumisos y rendidos
> Del Redentor el lábaro triunfante.
>
> El ha borrado con su sangre pura,
> La culpa que en la tierra cometisteis;
> Y abierto nuevamente a la criatura
> El inmortal Eden que aquí perdisteis. (90)

The serpent tempts Eve by describing the social, political, and educational benefits of the fruit. Eve is reluctant, unsure as to whether she should trust the animal, but accepts after becoming spellbound by Satan. Adam, seeing his wife with the fruit, wants to know how she dare disobey God. She explains the benefits of knowledge, talent, and power, and Adam succumbs without question. The Fall is described in images expressing moral decay: war, hate, pride, vengeance;

and nature is disrupted: shadows fill the earth, mountains and rivers weep, the animals wail. The poet then addresses atheists, so that they may learn from this tale.

God calls out from Heaven blaming Adam for corrupting the world. Adam blames Eve, and she blames the Serpent. God condemns the three, then offers clothes to the humans. Stating to himself that Adam has become like "one of us," God decides to teach the humans a lesson by sending them out of the garden. Recounting the many things that he had done for the humans, the Almighty expresses to them his disbelief that they would turn against him. He no longer recognizes the beings that he created and he expresses his anger and rejects them. Adam and Eve begin to cry, and the poet explains to his sad characters that the only remedy is to ask for pardon. He asks the angels to pray for Adam and Eve, but instead an angel descends and expels the pair from the garden.

Eve complains that the promises made by the serpent did not materialize, then laments the loss of innocence, remembering the company of God, the wonders of the garden, and their happiness. Eve asks God to forgive them. The Angel of Exculpation descends and pardons the humans, announcing that the Son will descend to Earth to give his life for their sin. Adam admits that they are not worthy of God's pity, but it is accepted and the pair have renewed hope that God is not so far away. The poet contemplates his own sinful state and mentions that, thanks to the Son, he will be with God since death has been conquered and the soul, coming from Heaven will return to Heaven.

All of the literary and dramatic adaptations of the Adamic myth reflect to some degree the socio-cultural environment in which they were composed. Of all the Adamic texts that have been examined so far, Rosselló's is extraordinary because of the manner in which it invests the Adamic myth with an editorial, almost propagandistic stance. While Lista and Reinoso emphasized the character of Satan in imitation of Milton, Rosselló chose to concentrate on the relationship between God and the humans, a relationship that would have to be drawn in human, not cosmic terms, for the Jahwist and the Spanish mystics had been powerful precedents. The Patriarchal fathers of the Church had interpreted the transgression of God's commandment as a breach in the ideal relationship that they imagined had existed between God and the first humans. Almost two thousand years after the Jahwist had written down the tale of Adam and Eve, Rosselló attempted to portray his imaginary version of the ideal relationship between God and human beings, and the result is detrimental to the Genesis myth and its orthodox notion of God.

Rosselló's God is the perfect image of the stern patriarch, but the poet gives a new turn to this Jahwehesque figure. This God is the most human God drawn from the figure of Jahweh, an Almighty who actively visits his children in paradise, walking in the garden with them "Dejando de sus pies, la huella impresa, / En sus prados, eternos, florecientes" (61); and God speaks to them "con habla siempre nueva, / Y acentos, de la tierra nunca oidos" (62). While all the literary artists had previously depicted God as the fierce God of the Old Testament and as the merciful Deity with the figures of Christ, Rosselló portrayed his Creator with a sentimental nature. After the pair have transgressed his command, God, in disbelief, laments that the humans have betrayed him: "Por vosotros formé esta morada, / Tan pura, tan gentil, tan deliciosa; / Por mí y mis serafines visitada, / Ved hoy ¡cuán triste está! ¡cuán pesarosa!" (110). And this is a lonely deity, for he reminisces about the days that he spent in the company of the humans:

> ¡Cuántas veces, os dije, desdichados,
> No olvideis mis preceptos y ley santa;
> Y que habeis sido por mis manos creados;
> Y vuestra ingratitud al sol espanta!
>
> ¡Cuántas veces, cual Padre cariñoso,
> En hablar con vosotros me gozaba,
> Y con los rayos de mi rostro hermoso
> Vuestra bella mansión iluminaba. (111)

Rosselló's God becomes angry, then he regrets loosing his temper. This overly personified figure of God, modeled on the walking, talking Jahweh of Genesis B, points out the functional aspects of the Adamic myth as a foundational story of Christianity.

Regarding the functional aspect of myth and the idea of myth as an expression of the culturally important information that a society wishes to preserve, this text is of interest for the way in which the poet treats his subject matter and the manner in which he directs his discourse to his reader. Rosselló's poem may be considered an effort to revitalize a Biblical myth which had become relatively unimportant to certain segments of society. In light of the declaration of independence from God resulting from the rise of skepticism towards the Bible in the nineteenth century by intellectuals such as Karl Marx, Charles Darwin, Friedrich Nietzsche and Sigmund Freud, Christianity found itself again taking up a defensive position against dissenters. *La caída de Adán* may be read as a defense of the veracity of the Genesis story, an attempt to infuse the story with signs pointing out its "truthfulness," and it appears specifically directed at those who would profess their doubt of the Gospels, namely, intellectuals, artist, and scientists. Doty has pointed out that there are three phases in the "vitality" of myth: the Primary myth addresses the needs of the culture by answering questions about existence. Then comes a stage which he calls implicit myth, where the story has become accepted and orthodox. Finally, the Rationalized myth comes about when the material that the myth expresses has been abstracted, or expressed in rationalized terms in order to conserve it and protect it from antagonizing elements (50). Obviously the importance of myths to society changes over time. The Primary stage of the Adamic myth must have occurred near the story's creation. By the time the tale was written by the Jahwist, it was already at the stage of implicit myth: this was the tale that told the beginning of evil in the world. After the Adamic myth had been edited by the Priestly writers, it was impossible to rationalize the content of the story, and centuries of speculative material resulted from attempts to understand the enigmas of the tale. Myths inevitably lose their meaning, their cultural relevance, since the society that sanctions their meaning changes. Concerning the erosion of the meaning of myth, Doty writes:

> Originally metaphors and symbols convey new, world-creative perceptions that resound with many different voices and meanings. We speak poetically or metaphorically when [language] does not allow us the necessary linguistic flexibility to state what is just coming into view. However, by repeated usage, metaphors and symbols become locked into single-meaning codes, where each term "stands for" only one meaning. Then, instead of opening up multiple insights, they close down alternative viewings and demand social conformity of usage. (21)

Because it could not be rationalized or expressed in more contemporary language, the Adamic myth became fossilized in a group of figures, incidents, and symbols that could mean nothing more than those that Christian ideology had previously accepted. Myths that once may have offered moral examples, when resurrected in later times, tend to function or serve as entertainment or adornment. As Christian myths were in the process of losing prestige for contemporary society, in the nineteenth century, the Biblical stories were agonizing from the conflict that ensued when the orthodox interpretations of the Bible came under the scrutiny of the ever more rational and objective minds.

With regard to the socio-cultural function of the myth of the Fall during the latter part of the seventeenth century, the creation story continued to serve as a viable cultural myth. The hierarchical structure of life that viewed humanity as dominated by a patriarchal God, the notion of humans as inferior and culpable beings who had been denied a formerly superior state and an idyllic existence of harmony because of the transgression of a sacrosanct precept were still considered the foundational lessons of the unalienable and consecrated "history" of the beginning of the world. Nevertheless, the effects of an increasing reliance on the rational examination of the physical world would lead scientists and philosophers to begin to question formerly inviolate truths. In time, an uneasy balance between faith in the "sacred" truths of the Bible and an increasing scientific observation of the physical world would lead to the rejection of the Church and its apocalyptic view of life. Just as the Classical worldview had faded into the past with the advent of monotheism, so Christianity, with its rigid belief system, could not meet the challenges of rational scrutiny, the emergence of positivism, and the growing desire for freedom of the individual. In order to better understand and gauge the European's changing perception of the Bible and its creation stories, the evolution of the notion of God against the backdrop of the rise of secularism may be used as a barometer.

After the Council of Trent, a renewed interest in the Scriptures coincided with the proliferation of the Adamic theme in art, drama and poetry. Acolytes of both reformist and Counter-Reformist persuasion began to perceive the Scriptures as the literal word of God. The conflict between the Church's staunch defense of the Bible as literal truth and a new faith in the individual's power of observation as a basis of truth would eventually begin to unravel the Biblical myths. If the seventeenth century had seen an increasing faith and reliance on the Bible as a literal document, the thinkers of the Enlightenment found themselves turning increasingly outward to the lessons learned from the objective analysis of nature, and inward to an increasing reliance on the judgment of the individual for the answers to the ultimate questions of the universe. When Christians began to view their faith in light of the new scientific methods, some came to the conclusion that God can only be known by contemplating the world. The objective analysis of religion ignored the metaphorical and symbolic nature of the writings. As scientific ojectivism might be irrelevant to art or poetry, the Bible was subjected to rational critique because it was thought to be a literal document. The consequences were severe for religion: "Western Christians were now committed to a literal understanding of their faith and had taken an irrevocable step back from myth: a story was either factually true or it was a delusion" (Armstrong 307). For a God that was supposedly revealed in historical events, the discrepancies between the Bible and empirical evidence would lead many to discount the veracity of the Scriptures. In time, the philosophers of the Enlightenment would begin to question the truthfulness of their traditional beliefs. Rationalism and the growing secularization of society had a profound effect on the Europeans' view of religion and the Bible. At the end of the European Enlightenment, philosophers would begin to postulate the demise of the Biblical God.

Positivism was another ingredient in the evolution of the western idea of God. A more optimistic view of the world was discordant with the Scriptures. By the end of the eighteenth century, the West was exerting an ever increasing influence on the rest of the world in the realms of science and the technicalization of society. In the newly emerging technical society, change and the myth of progress became culturally important substitutes for the view of the universe as a place of suffering, where life only served to prepare one to enter the "true life" in heavenly union with God. Optimism about the relation of humanity to nature and a new confidence in the individual's ability to achieve enlightenment by means of personal effort were in direct opposition to Medieval notions of God as the wrathful, yet merciful Supreme Being. Thanks to the optimism afforded by the progress of science, societies arrived at a new, confident relation with nature, to the point that people "no longer felt that they needed to rely on inherited tradition, an institution or an elite—or, even, a revelation from God— to discover truth" (Armstrong 296).

Rosselló's poem demonstrates the erosion of the Adamic myth's vitality, because it exhibits a number of factors that serve to re-invest the story with meaning. The lengthy invocation sets the tone for the poem and gives the reader a unequivocal indication of the moral posture of the poet and the Romantic effusiveness of his religious expression. The poet is unrestrained in his zeal to demonstrate his belief in God, and he presents an almost endless string of hyperbolic images pointing out the profound love he feels for God and his equally profound disdain for the world: "Deseo que en mis versos se refleje, / El amor que mi alma te profesa: / Nada importa que el mundo se me aleje: / El mundo ha de cesar; tu amor no cesa" (9). Asking for inspiration from God in order to tell the sad tale of Adam and Eve, the poet states that his only ambition is to love God eternally (9); that the world may think him insane, but he will always yearn for his Lord. At one point, the poet writes in imitation of Bécquer: "Mi poesía eres

Tú. Tu luz me envía / El raudal de armonía que hervir siento / En el seno in- mortal del alma mía, / Inundando de luz mi entendimiento" (10). Rosselló's disdain for the world is presented with imagery expression a profound solitude that can only be relieved in the company of God: "Triste vivo en el mundo, sin consuelo, / Todo huye de mí y me abandona; / Más ¿qué importa, si Tú tienes un cielo / Para mi alma inmortal y una corona? (11). In expressing his love for God, he projects his sentiment onto nature:

> Te adoro, cual tus astros celestiales,
> Cual la aurora, de perlas coronada;
> Cual el mar, que la copia en sus cristales,
> Cual el sol, que refleja tu mirada.
>
> Te adoro, cual te adoran esas nubes,
> Vestidas de topacio o amaranto;
> Que al Angel, acaso, o los querubes,
> Sirven de tienda o primoroso manto. (11)

These are the major motifs that are repeated in the first eighty strophes of the Invocation. It is here also that we find one of the messages that motivate Rosselló's poem, namely, a desire or need to sing the praises of God's grandeur:

> Nunca, nunca mi alma cesaría
> De cantar en tu nombre y alabanza,
> Hasta que su destierro trocaría
> Por tu patria feliz de su esperanza.
>
> A cantar voy ora, pues, tus maravillas,
> Tu gloria, tu saber, tu poderío;
> Estrellas, luna y sol, de vuestras sillas,
> Atentos escuchad el canto mío. (19)

Rosselló uses the figure of Adam, and to a lesser extent, Eve, as examples of correct attitude and behavior towards God. The first man is described as a free and intelligent being, the culmination of the Creation, a beautiful creature formed to serve as the "voice of love" to God (23). We are told that the first humans enjoy free will, except, as God aptly points out, the humans owe him "fiel obediencia, / Adoración suprema, ilimitada: / Por haberos dotado de existencia, /sacándoos del seno de la nada" (39). This poem's Adam faithfully does as he is commanded: "Bendito seas, Señor, eternamente, / . . . / Todo ser, toda luz, todo viviente, / Ensálcente sin fin, loen tu nombre" (45), until Eve asks him to eat. While Adam serves as a positive example of how to relate to God, the figure of Satan is minimized in the poem. Possessing only negative qualities, and no sympathetic attributes, Rosselló's Satan is the horrendous serpent, or the rebellious angel, and is described as a "monstruo deforme" with a barbed tail with sparks and flames flowing from his eyes (77-78). But the figure only appears during the temptation and in a brief interlude afterward, a flashback, in which the poet relates the hellish machination.

The poet's digressions in the narrative constitute one of the most characteristic features of *La caída de Adán*. This poet, overwhelmed by his love for God and an equally robust aversion to life on Earth, seems most anxious to publicize his religiosity. The poet's imagery is excessively worn and hackneyed at its best, and propagandistic at its worst. At times Rosselló interjects thoughts, feelings, and warnings into the text: while describing Eden, the poet asks mortals to weep for the "insanity" of the first humans (26); during the temptation episode, Eve is warned about the serpent awaiting her (72); after the creation of Eve, the poet exhorts the angels to admire Eve's beauty (47), or he addresses her directly, warning her not to transgress God's will. After Adam and Eve have eaten the fruit, he asks the angels to pray that God forgive the humans (72-73). The intrusion of a poet's voice into the narrative is not usually a disruptive feature per se, but given a story that is as well known as the Genesis B, the comments take on an amusing air, especially regarding the poet's direct exhortations to his characters. For example, in asking that the Angels intervene to stop Eve from tasting the fruit, the emotionally charged statement directed towards a character whose actions are completely predictable becomes comically insincere.

Rosselló's emotional editorializing is most evident in the climactic episode of the piece, after the episode of the Fall, where the poet interrupts the narration to warn those who do not adhere to his religious beliefs about the consequences of their ideology. It is here that the conflict between the poet's religiosity and the erosion of the myth of the Fall is most evident. As the world is changed by the sin of Adam and Eve, the poet speaks to non-believers:

> Ateos, aprended en este ejemplo,
> Vosotros que de Dios negais la esencia,
> Y de la gloria y el saber al templo,
> Todos quereis llegar, sin su asistencia.

Mirad de nuestra madre la caída,
Por haber, cual vosotros, escuchado
Del orgullo la sierpe maldecida,
Y de Dios los enojos provocado.

Cayó como la estrella esplendorosa,
Que de los cielos en la frente brilla;
La pura, bella, y encendida rosa,
Señora del Eden, perdió su silla.

También ella subir, rebelde, quiso,
Del saber a la cumbre soberana:
Costóle su osadía un paraíso.
Y el castigo de Dios. ¡Locura insana! (101)

Rosselló attempts to revitalize the myth by reinvesting it with a literal meaning so that it might function as a moral guide for those whose system of belief does not encompass the myth or its deity. Then he accuses the philosophers that would deny his religion. The poet begins his diatribe against science, suggesting that nature is the proof of God's existence.

Sin Dios la ciencia ¿qué es? Triste camino,
De abismos y de abrojos todo lleno,
Demencia, ceguedad y desatino,
Dorada copa de mortal veneno.

¿No veis esas esferas esplendentes,
Tan altas, tan serenas y espaciosas;
No es verdad que iluminan vuestras mentes,
Consuelan vuestras almas angustiosas? (102)

The poet then describes the beauty of nature, the beauty of the Creation, and follows with a condemnation of science:

¿Quisierais, pues, vosotros, hombres ciegos,
Desviar de Dios los ojos y la mente,
Negarle vuestro culto y vuestros ruegos,

De la ciencia, sin El, hallar la fuente?

Dejaos de soñar mas desatinos,
Alzad vuestra mirada al Ser supremo;
El origen del mundo y los destinos
No ha de variar vuestro clamor blasfemo.
        (103)

It is the investigation of nature, or the search for truth in the individual's experience of nature, that has led to the erosion of the meaning or the cultural significance of the old myths. The last quartet is most ironic, for the command that the atheists stop their delusions might best be directed at the poet, who would have the late nineteenth century accept as meaningful a version of the history of the world that was no longer accepted by well-informed persons. This is the voice of one defending his belief against threats of extinction. The poem's extremely moralizing tone, its abuse of hackneyed Biblical imagery, its abuse of digression, the poet's voice as commentator, and finally its excessively defensive stance against those whose ideas would threaten the poet's beliefs seem to point to the fact that the poet needed to fill a cultural vacuum by writing this text. The age of science had found a new religion and thanks to Darwin's *The Origin of Species* (1859), there were new creation "myths" circulating. Scientific objectivity had replaced Rosselló's creation story and, thus, the poet's zealous position in defense of his faith had been eroded even prior to his understanding.

Since Milton represented an aesthetic inspiration rather than a direct influence on Lista and Reinoso, their poems on the theme of lost innocence were molded by their ideal notions of the poet Milton and his *Paradise Lost*. It appears that neither poet had a complete knowledge of Milton's poem at the time of the writing of each version of "La inocencia perdida" therefore the poets were not discouraged by the daunting example of their English model. They each proceeded to copy the genre, the tone, the overall structural format followed by Milton—beginning the Creation story with the "prehistorical" rebellion of the Angels, and thus, depicting the Fall of the humans as an extension of the battle between absolute good and absolute evil—and they followed Milton's "classical" example by composing a work that combined a moral lesson with the supreme example of the most "august" literary genre, the epic. With regards to the theological expression of the works, unlike Milton who portrayed his God as completely omniscient of the Fall of both Satan and man, the Spanish poets portrayed the figure of Satan as a true rebel against God, and thus, they continued the tradition of the Church's insistence on the value of free will, and the use of the Adamic myth as an expression of the wrongful use of the will.

Written some seventy years later, Rosselló's *La caída de Adán* appears to be a response to aesthetic trends also. I have read this poem as a defense of Christianity against the new theories of science and philosophy that were beginning to deny God a place in the natural world, but, the poem was also a reaction against the Spanish manifestations of liberal Romanticism, which, as Lista had noted, sought to inculcate an immoral, and even anti-religious lesson. Like the poems from the Seville school, Rosselló's poem illustrates that the poet continued the long tradition of utilizing the Adamic myth to teach a moral lesson about the severed relationship between humanity and God. These early modern literary versions of the Adamic myth continued the tradition of portraying humanity's metaphysical dilemma as based on an outdated, overlysimplified model that pitted absolute evil against the ultimate benevolent Deity, with humans caught up in the struggle between opposite camps.

# Chapter Four:

## *El diablo mundo* and the Subversion
## of the Adamic Myth

*El diablo mundo* appeared some twenty years earlier than Rosselló's *La caída de Adán*. Nevertheless, I have chosen to deal with this text lastly as a separate but related part of the study, because it is the most complex of the works to be considered, and because, unlike the other plays and poems included, Espronceda's poem is not an obvious attempt to retell the Adamic myth. When *El diablo mundo* was published on the seventh of October, 1840, it was declared the most important contemporary poem written in Castilian (Casalduero *Forma* 15). Despite the poem's narrative departure from the Adamic myth, the nature of Espronceda's hero and the manner in which Espronceda utilized elements from the Adam and Eve myth justify the inclusion of *El diablo mundo* in this study of the Spanish Adamic tradition. This work represents a decidedly Romantic treatment of the Genesis A and B material.

It is well known that Espronceda's poem gave rise to much debate as to the sources and the manner in which the poet might have been influenced, especially by Byron, Goethe's *Faust*, and possibly Voltaire's *L'Ingénu*. José Moreno Villa viewed Espronceda's Adam as a combination of Faust and Candide, and Américo Castro, in his article "Acerca de *El diablo mundo* de Espronceda," perceives the critical attitude of the poem as a reflection of eighteenth century France. Although he points out many similarities between *El diablo mundo* and *L'Ingenu*, he does not suggest that Espronceda was influenced directly by Voltaire's novel. Francisco Caravaca has noted numerous secondary influences — Musset, Hugo, Lamartine, Quinet, and even Calderón— who may have informed the work as well.[1] Alessandro Martinengo addresses the problem of influence in his close reading of the poem, *Polimorfismo nel "Diablo mundo" d'Espronceda*. This critic points out Espronceda's originality in his creation of a multifarious poem, combining a variety of styles, themes, timbres and rhythms. Confirming that the poem is unique to Espronceda, Martinengo states that ultimately the work derives its humor from Byron, and its metaphysical nature from Goethe. This idea is confirmed by Robert Marrast, who notes that the poem was conceived:

como obra destinada a ser una versión española, pero en ningún caso una imitación servil, del *Faust* de Goethe y del *Manfred* or el *Caín* de Byron, combinando en una síntesis original los aspectos visionarios de la primera con el titanismo y el humorismo sarcástico de las segundas, y pasando progresivamente del mundo de las ideas puras al de la realidad, incluso de la más sórdida. (58)

Much less attention has been given to the similarities between Gracián's *El criticón* and Espronceda's poem. Adolfo Bonilla y San Martín is probably the first to mention the idea of *El criticón* as a possible source for *El diablo mundo*, and he states that the Romantic poem might have had an older precedent in Albucháfar Abentofáil (d. 1185), in whose twelfth-century novel, *El viviente, hijo del vigilante*, there appears a hero possessing qualities similar those of Andrenio and Adán:

[El héroe] viene al mundo y llega al uso de la razón sin lenguaje articulado, que poco a poco va dándose cuenta de los problemas y dolores de la vida, y a quien también incita a meditar el espectáculo de la muerte. Reproduce luego la misma idea un moralista ilustre de nuestra patria . . . , Baltasar Gracián . . . , cuyo Andrenio se parece extraordinariamente al Adán de Espronceda. (96-97)

Soon after, Castro refuted this suggestion, basing his argument on the enormous differences in "el espíritu y el sentido" of the two works (375). Nevertheless, there are many interesting similarities between *El criticón* and *El diablo mundo* with regards to the nature of their heroes: the introduction of mature but inexperienced characters into society, whereby the education of the innocent serves to differentiate the initiated from the uninitiated, setting the stage for moral or social criticism; the creation of characters that represent the collective human experience and that embody the Thomistic union of opposites of spirit and matter; a critical and pessimistic view of life; and the use of the pilgrimage motif.

While Castro did not elaborate upon his discussion of the spirit and sense of the two works, the differences are obvious. Gracián, like Espronceda, takes as his point of departure a corrupt world and places within it a candid being representing an idealized state of naturalness, uncorrupted and unindoctrinated by human society. Nevertheless, the didacticism of Gracián's novel, most notable in the complexity and consistency of the allegorical structure, and in the sententiousness aimed at the preservation of its true hero—the seventeenth-century individual—could not be farther from Espronceda's acerbic investigation into the nature of humanity's metaphysical condition. One fundamental difference between *El criticón* and *El diablo mundo* is that in the former, the individual, guided by adequate knowledge and the use of critical reasoning, can find a way to cope with the pervasive deceptions of an imperfect world. But it must be pointed out that Gracián's world is one that is still watched over by a perfect Creator. On the other hand, in focusing attention on the injustice of life and in seeking the source of human suffering, Espronceda can only express doubt and criticism towards the omnipotent Creator. God's silence and inaction with regard to the pain, loneliness, and death of his creation can only be perceived by the Romantic artist as illogical, if not hostile. While a more thorough contrastive study of *El criticón* and *El diablo mundo* is beyond the scope of this investigation, a study of the figure of Andrenio can help to shed light on Espronceda's Adán, the relationship of Adán to the Adamic myth, and the use of the myth in *El diablo mundo*.

In an article concerning politics and anthropology in Gracián's work, José Antonio Maravall has studied what he calls the "adamismo" of the figure of Andrenio, in which he states that the Adamic aspect of the figure is essential to an understanding of *El criticón* and to the philosophy of Gracián as well. Investigating the epistemological processes that may have guided Gracián's use of an Adamic figure, Maravall views the character of Andrenio, the unexperienced, candid, and instinctual man, as an extension of seventeenth-century rationalist thought, where, in order to penetrate more complex structures, the processes of analysis and speculation lead to simplification:

> Hay en el pensamiento moderno, desde su origen y en todo el pensamiento racionalista del XVII, una tendencia a analizar la realidad para buscar los elementos simples de que está formada. En Bacon, en Descartes, en Locke, esa tendencia es bien clara y sobradamente conocida. A esa orientación analítica de la realidad y de la vida, responde el procedimiento de Gracián, reduciendo el hombre a su simplicidad originaria, analizándolo en sus puros elementos y presentándonoslo como un Adán que, paso a paso, reconstruye la complejidad de la existencia. A ese afán por descomponer la realidad en busca de lo simple, tratando de partir de los supuestos primitivos para penetrar en fases posteriores y dominar la complejidad con que hoy se nos presentan las cosas, pertenece, en el plano de la investigación de lo humano, el in-

cremento del tema 'adánico' que podemos fácilmente observar en la
época. (351)

This distinguished critic goes on to qualify his reference to Adam. He
points out the difference between Adam of the Original Sin and the notion of
Adam as "new" man, who exists as a part of the natural world and, nevertheless, is completely unfettered by the social, historical and cultural confines of
human society. Andrenio is a being, adds Maravall, who is imperfect as a consequence of his humanity:

> Gracián pretende dejar aparte, provisionalmente, claro está, lo que la
> historia, la sociedad y la cultura han depositado sobre el hombre, para
> buscar el estrato primario que ha permanecido en él, sin que aquéllas
> puedan nunca anularlo. Y no pretende con esto suprimir esas capas
> posteriores, sino penetrar mejor en su sentido y organizar más
> adecuadamente la vida humana y social. Gracián parte de las posibili-
> dades adánicas que conservamos siempre en el fondo, para replantear
> el problema de nuestra vida personal y de nuestro puesto en la so-
> ciedad. Dada la esfera de autonomía moral de la persona en que antes
> vimos se mueve el autor, ese hombre primario que en estado química-
> mente puro nos presenta, no es un Adán pecador, sino un Adán imper-
> fecto. No hay en él —porque no le interesa, dado el plano en que se de-
> senvuelve su análisis— un primer hombre al que se le haya de imputar
> una falta históricamente cometida, sino un hombre primario, que, en su
> pura humanidad, pasa por la necesaria y constante caída de su imper-
> fección. (352-53)

José Antonio Maravall's observation, which regards the character as a consequence of rationalist thinking, is well formed; however, the analogy of Andrenio with Adam is not entirely accurate given the fact that the figure of Adam
is inseparably linked to the notion of the Fall in seventeenth-century Spain. As I
have shown earlier, the notion of "Adam" entails the conceptual baggage of
centuries of interpretive writings focusing on the figure in its religious context,
and therefore, the notion of an "Adán imperfecto" can only lead us back to the
postlapsarian first man, in which case we must speak of the Adam of the first
sin, "Adán pecador."

It is more accurate to consider the character of Andrenio in relation to the
natural world. Unlike the prelapsarian Adam who is hierarchically superior to

the animal world, Andrenio is more closely related to his "animal" nature. In his analysis of Andrenio, Theodore L. Kassier relates that throughout Gracián's novel, the figure never loses its link to the natural world, and this is evident in that Andrenio embodies both the "brutishness and irrationality of the wild animals," and simutaneously the candid "benevolence" of the inexperienced (13). Raised among the wild animals on the island of Saint Helena, the character's sudden release leads to what Kassier calls the "overwhelming sensual infatuation" with the phenomena of nature. As a consequence, the figure exhibits an "insatiable curiosity, propelled and partially defined by instinctual and brutish exuberance" (13). The combination of sensual instinctiveness (irrationality) and innocence, says Kassier, may seem ambiguous:

> On the one hand [Andrenio] embodies a candid idealism and natural-
> ness reminiscent of the fabled 'Edad de oro' extolled by Don Quixote
> . . . . On the other hand, he embodies an irrational sensuality devoted to
> satisfying brutish instinct, a hungry curiosity suggestive of the *pícaro's*
> excesses, but without the *pícaro's* purposeful depravity and cynical
> view. Ultimately, he personifies a natural and artless perspective unre-
> strained by critical judgment or the caution of experience, an instinc-
> tive point of view governed only by the physical senses, perceiving and
> appreciating only the superficial sensual aspects of reality and judging
> exclusively on the basis of appearance, and thus susceptible to entrap-
> ment by the invitations to vice prevalent in the unnatural world men
> have created beyond the boundaries of Saint Helena's pristine perfec-
> tion. (14-15)

While Andrenio's instinctual curiosity about life and his intimate relationship with the natural world is suggestive of the prelapsarian state of the first humans where Adam and Eve existed in harmony with the animals, and where Eve's innate curiosity led to their disobedience of God, it is not appropriate to associate Andrenio with the idea of paradise.

While the notions of primitivism, the Golden Age, and Eden are similar concepts, a clarification is in order so as not to confuse these ideas. The concept of an idyllic people inhabiting a paradisiacal place is of unknown origin; however, the manifestations of the idea in Western art and literature are not infrequent and can be traced to the earliest Greek and Near Eastern literatures. Through the ages the paradise myth, like the myths of the *Saturnia Regna* (the Golden Age of man), and the Noble Savage, has been a hallmark of humanity's awareness of self within the broader context of society and civilization. Living within the confines of a social group, the complications of coexistence may become unbearable, and the individual yearns for a simpler life, an escape from the repressive complexities of the contemporary world. Dreams of paradise, of Arcadia, of Eden and Heaven are specific examples of the universal fantasy about the ideal existence in a place far removed from the present circumstances by time, space, or both. Whether the dreams are projected into the past, as in the case of earthly paradises, the nobler ages, or the pre-lapsarian Eden; or whether visions are projected into the future, as are the progressivistic dreams of pastoral or urban utopias and heavenly afterlives, it seems that these paradisiacal legacies of earlier cultures are the pronounced manifestations of humanity's physical and/or metaphysical discontent. The quotidian grind of the contemporary experience simply does not resemble the imagined bountiful garden or the blissful tranquillity of "Golden" times where an earlier people existed in harmony with all of nature's elements and free from life's travails.

The fantasy of humanity's paradise lost may give rise to apotheosis (the exaltation of a lost paradisiacal condition), as in the case of the Golden Age, or it may, as in the case of the Adamic myth, serve an etiological function telling us what might have been in order to explain or lament the present. Richard Heinberg, who has studied the universal myth of paradise lost, finds that the basic metaphor at the heart of the myth is the search for happiness, but there are differences between the Greek and the Hebraic models. As Heinberg points out,

> the Golden Age has never acquired the puritanical overlays associated with the Eden narrative. Indeed, the naturalistic primitivist poets of the Counter-Renaissance —Pierre de Tonsard, Torquato Tasso, and John Donne— went so far as to extol the Golden Age as a time of free expression of the sexual impulse, a time when love had no 'regiment,' when human beings were free to follow their essentially healthy natural instincts. (191)

Related to the myth of paradise is the idea of Primitivism, which is the basis of our concept of the Noble Savage, and which also expresses a dissatisfaction with the here and now. According to Alex Preminger, the primitivist takes as the models for life the earlier cultures that existed or may have existed in the past, or from less sophisticated, or more "primitive" peoples still living. The mind of the child and the "psychologically elemental (subrational or even subconscious) level of existence" also serve to express primitivistic ideals (663). Given the instinctual brutishness and the insatiable curiosity of Andrenio, the figure is closer to the notion of primitivism than to the Greek or Hebrew models of paradise.

Nevertheless, according to the research of M. L. Welles, Primitivism and Paradise may be inaccurate concepts by which to understand Gracián's use of the figure. In a study of the myth of the Golden Age in *El criticón*, Welles makes it clear that the Golden Age appears in the epic novel only as an expression of negative contrast. In other words, instead of portraying the benefits and positive characteristics of a previous Golden time, Gracián highlights what was missing in the earlier ages: war, malice, and deceit. Any positive notion or idealization of the past is excluded (390). Regarding Primitivism, Wells notes that Gracián is an anti-primitivist in his estimation of man's instinctive being, for the world for Gracián is "a sorry state of post-lapsarian corruption, inhabited by bestial men" (391). Paradoxically, as Welles aptly points out, the corrupt world in Gracián's novel does not originate from a transgression of God's law, and the notion of an original sin as an excuse for the "weakened" state of humanity is ostensibly missing from the work (391).

In addition, for all the attention given to the corruption and moral decay of the world, the notion of religion as a means of future salvation is virtually absent as well. Critilo and Andrenio (representing "*todos los mortales*") fail in their search for Felisenda, and at the end of their epic journey we do not find any references to the Christian notion of paradise; but rather, the Island of Immortality teaches Andrenio that the only effective remedy against death is memory. As Kassier points out:

> [Critilo's and Andrenio's] reward for having successfully negotiated life's hazardous pilgrimage, and the antidote against death, . . . is not the Christian salvation whose absence has troubled critics since the work was written. Rather it is the immortality of preservation in men's memories, the secular but nonetheless everlasting glory of the hero. (30)

Maravall reaches the same conclusion regarding the "secular" nature of the work: Gracián does not lead his "individual" of instinct and reason to contemplate the religious life nor is the Church a problem to be addressed. Gracián is not extolling a Christian virtue, rather the virtue of the hero, the man of action (343-44).

While Gracián excludes the notion of a past or future redemption, the Christian context is not entirely absent from the work, for it functions as an ideological background. Gracían can only perceive the world as a part of God's creation where man's natural inclination is to know and love God, and God manifests his presence to man through the creation.

> —Es muy connatural —dixo Critilo— en el hombre la inclinación a su Dios, como a su principio y su fin, ya amándole, ya conociéndole. [. . .] Dios hay que es su norte, centro y sol a quien busque, en quien pare y a quien goze. Este gran Señor dio el ser a todo lo criado, mas él de sí mismo le tiene, y aun por esso es infinito en todo género de perfección, que nadie le pudo limitar ni el ser, ni el lugar, ni el tiempo. No se ve, pero se conoce; y, como soberano Príncipe, estando retirado a su inaccessible incomprehensibilidad, nos habla por medio de sus criaturas. (95)

Neither the perfected states of the past nor possibility of a paradisiacal future seem to concern Gracián in his work. Neither is he reformist in his moral stance. On the contrary, according to Maravall, Gracián is most in tune with his Jesuit training, his philosophy, and his epoch when he demonstrates disdain for utopian thought and reformers. His is literature that "[n]o pretende cambiar de raíz el estado de cosas criticando, sino analizarlo y exponer su condición, para dar al individuo, que es irrenunciablemente parte de esa sociedad, una técnica de acomodación," a characteristic, notes Maravall, that is common to European literature of a moral and political nature in this epoch (340-41). Instead of attempting to transform society by presenting his criticism of the moral conduct of society, notes Maravall, Gracián is advocating a conservatism based on the individual: "[e]l culto gracianesco del héroe tiene un carácter conservador: el héroe es, en él, un factor de establilización. Y su justificación moral está en que precisamente él, el héroe, el eminente, es quien saca a la luz, con su ejemplo, las posibilidades éticas que en la sociedad, tal como existe, se contienen" (341).

The lack of any exaltation of a lost paradise, of any notion of Original Sin, and of any reformist tendencies in the work should lead us away from the association of Andrenio with the prelapsarian Adam. The absence of references to Primitivism and the limited use of the myth of the Golden Age suggest that the figure is not related to the Greek model of paradise. A more accurate term to describe the character might be "neophyte," for the actions of Andrenio and his alter ego Critilo represent more closely the initiation of a novice. Andrenio is a pure being only in that he has not been corrupted by contact with humans, and thus, in this sense, he retains his virtue despite his human imperfection: "Dichoso tú que te criaste entre las fieras . . . que entre los hombres, pues cada uno es un lobo para el otro" (I 98). The figure is not a first man in the sense that Adam is a first man; we should view Andrenio as an "uncivilized" figure, in the sense that he was previously not of the human community, and thus, a figure who will not think, perceive, nor act in a preconditioned (civilized) manner. Andrenio is an uninitiated whose actions will serve to highlight, to throw new light on, the subject of Gracián's work, which is life; thus Critilo tells Andrenio that he envies his "privilegio único del primer hombre y tuyo: llegar a ver con novedad y con advertencia la grandeza, la hermosura, el concierto, la firmeza y la variedad desta gran máquina criada" (I 77). In the contrast between the "uninitiated" (Andrenio) and the "initiated" (Critilo), between the "neophyte" and the "veteran" is where Gracián bases his moral criticism of society and offers his philosophy to successfully navigate life's deception. Andrenio is not an Adamic figure, at least in the Judeo-Christian sense which has been the focus of this study. Gracián avoids the Biblical first man, according to Maravall, because it would have given him less autonomy. It had less possibility as a character in the allegorical sense. Thus he chose a figure that represents a blank slate, a character of "naturaleza pura" who is unknowledgeable in the ways of the world and must be guided constantly by Critilo, his voice of reason (352). The focus on the imperfection of Andrenio means that there exists the possibility of reaching a state of perfection, and for that reason Critilo, the voice of reason, is placed at Andrenio's side, as a guide and instructor. In light of the previous outline of the characteristics of Gracián's Andrenio, the fact that Espronceda makes frequent references and allusions to the Genesis myths and its figures, to the notion of paradise, to immortality, and to the question of evil, would lead us to assume that Espronceda's character Adán appears to have more in common with his namesake than with Gracián's character.

This idea is reiterated by Francisco García Lorca, who, in his article "Espronceda y el paraíso," notes that in all the confusion as to Espronceda's influences, the most obvious source, the Genesis narration, has been overlooked. García Lorca aptly points out Espronceda's portrayal of God as the wrathful deity of the Old Testament and the poet's use of numerous "Edenic themes," which, the critic notes, point to the theme of the beginning of evil. But Espronceda's narrative sequence that recounts the transformation of the old man into Adán, and the subsequent incidents regarding Adán's initiation into society receive scant attention in García Lorca's article. This critic expresses that Espronceda had identified with Adam, but García Lorca fails to develop this idea further, except to vaguely suggest a relationship between the Romantics and the myth of the creation (225).

Joaquín Casalduero is more specific regarding Espronceda's use of the Adamic figure and its relation to the Romantics. In his *Forma y visión de* El diablo mundo *de Espronceda*, Casalduero explains that the Romantics had a penchant for Adam because the figure is an ideal metaphor for their cherished notion of individual liberty. Stating that the dominant trait of the Romantic is that he is first and foremost a rebel, as opposed to a titan, Casalduero clarifies the commitment and the identification of the Romantic artist with his rebellion, and as a consequence, with the figure of Adam:

> La rebelión expresa ya totalmente su personalidad, su deseo de ser él, su sentimiento adámico, esa necesidad de lo nuevo, esa necesidad de ser el primero, que es una manera de ser único. El hombre romántico no quiere ser un Fausto, sino un Adán; quiere libertarse de ese obstáculo que encuentra siempre en su camino: la historia, el pasado, el sentimiento de la culpa. Quiere librarse de la memoria que le sujeta y tortura, quiere matar el recuerdo que encadena al presente en su temporalidad. (27)

Like Gracián's character Andrenio, Espronceda wants to strip the human animal to its essential nature, to divest it of the ideological strata that result from the inculcation of history and culture by society. But the motives of the two artists are vastly different. Andrenio represents a simplification, a return to basics, a model depicting the encounter between the uninitiated (Andrenio) with the initiated (Critilo) so that the didactic purposes of his work, the *desengaño* of the individual, may be served. Espronceda's Adán is a return to the beginnings, a portrayal of man's innocent nature, not for the purpose of instructing how to negotiate one's way through the illusions of life, but because the innocence of Espronceda's Adán reflects negatively upon the established social order, and, more importantly, upon the cosmological order. It is in the primordial beginning, or more specifically, in the Christian beginning of history, that the ideological basis of society (history) derives its authority, and since the desire of the true Romantic is to annihilate authoritarianism, Espronceda returns to the Adamic figure and its myth as an ultimate expression of his rebellion against what he perceives to be the unjust laws of the universe.

García Lorca's analysis of the paradise motif in *El diablo mundo* represents a contribution to an area of research begun earlier by Vaclav Cerny, who in his article, "Quelques remarques sur les sentiments religieux chez Rivas et Espronceda," had studied Espronceda's poem as an attempt by the artist to deal with what the critic considers the most important theme of the poem, the notion of evil. Cerny's study contrasts Rivas ("très imbu de traditions religieuses nationales") with Espronceda, whom he describes as a soul torn apart with moral and sensitive contradictions. For Cerny, evil is the impetus for all of the action of Espronceda's poem and evil is the theme from which the poem derives its sense and its unity:

> On peut dire que la vie d'Adam, héros du poème esproncédien, n'est, depuis le moment où il s'éveille régénéré, immortel et sans le souvenir du passé ni connaissance de la vie, qu'une découverte progressive du mal. C'est un apprentissage de la douleur, de la douleur imméritée, bien entendu, car Espronceda suppose à priori l'âme de son Ingénu immaculée. (84)

Adán's innocence immediately conflicts with society where the eager and happy character learns that "no hay placer donde el dolor no quepa" (273), a lesson taught by *madrileños* with stones, knives, and imprisonment. But Espronceda places the blame for human cruelty on the figure of God as well. Goodness is a concept that is not found in Adán's world, notes Cerny, and the knowledge of death is presented in two examples of Hugoesque antithesis. The first antithesis is found in the scene in which the old woman mourns the death of her young daughter while in the adjacent room, others are having an orgy. The second example, writes Cerny, occurs when the desperate woman who is resigned to accept her bitter fate simply because it is God's will, is confronted with the naively confident air of Adán who assures her that God could not possibly deny her prayers to return life to the daughter's corpse. Cerny concludes that Espronceda is unique within Spain for having posed the problem of evil in his work, but while this problem is an "axe central de la personnalité religieuse d'Espronceda," Cerny states that the question, nevertheless, is left unresolved in *El diablo mundo*, unfinished as the poem is.

García Lorca's study provides a more complete analysis of the Adamic myth as an essential part of *El diablo mundo* by approaching the poem in its relation to the paradise theme, Original Sin, and, to a lesser extent, the problem of evil. According to this critic, Espronceda's unique notion of romantic love is the element that links the variety of "Edenic" themes evident in the poem, including the theme of the relationship between God and humanity. *El diablo mundo* expresses the notion that the God of Creation and the forces of Heaven condemn man to a hopeless life of suffering and are indifferent to his implorations, and this causes a sensation of solitude, a "desolada soledad del hombre ante la indiferencia de Dios" of which there are many examples in the poem. This condemnation of man repeats the Fall of Luzbel, and, as García Lorca correctly points out, the solidarity between man and Luzbel is expressed intensely in the poem (226).

The notion of love in *El diablo mundo*, continues García Lorca, is linked to the idea of impurity and death: "[h]ay en Espronceda una terrible idea angustiosa de que el amor degrada. Lo que más alto hace subir el espíritu del hombre, lo único que puede encender en él la chispa divina, lleva en sí, inevitable, el germen de la corrupción" (227). The "Canto a Teresa" is the most salient example of this "proceso de la pureza a la degradación" that seems to mark all of Espronceda's portrayal of women, and thus, notes the critic, the idea of Original Sin becomes a constant barrier for the attainment of pure love (227). A notion of love corrupted by the primal transgression against God links the concept of love to the "paradise" theme. García Lorca writes that the idealization of love, or love as a paradisiacal experience, can only lead to disillusionment in Espronceda's poem. The reason for this is that perfect love is impossible: "ese pecado original que al inficcionar los más nobles deseos e ilusiones del hombre hace de la vida misma un amargo delito" (228). The paradise of ideal love is impossible to find, but the possibility of "paradise regained" is a motive for the continual search for happiness that the experience of love might bring. The "memory" of the ideal love leads to renewed attempts to discover that blissful experience, and thus, Espronceda creates a circle of unfulfilled expectations in his characters where the male and female play out their search for the "lost paradise" of love, unable to escape the fatal consequences of the primordial contamination:

> Pero si el amor es imposible, el hombre no puede menos de buscarlo: la más alta virtud de la mujer es la ilusión de amor, del hombre, el impulso hacia su realización, aun conscientes ambos de su imposibilidad. La fuerza que arrastra a realizar una quimera de la que es imposible apartarse engendra un sentimiento desesperado en el que la razón desmiente constantemente al deseo. Dentro de este esquema, la mujer es una víctima fatal del hombre, ya que fuera de él la mujer, como mujer, no tiene existencia posible. Y el poeta se vuelve contra ella al

ver eternamente proyectada la sombra de la mujer primera, o la irri-
tación la resuelve en un sentimiento de piedad que abarca lo mismo a la
doncella alimentada por la pura ilusión de amor, que a la mujer ya
caída que va consumando su propio drama espoleada por el deseo. La
oscilación de sentimientos que el "Canto a Teresa" trasluce es típico.
(230-31)

García Lorca's assessment of love as a lost paradise that leads to embittered
disillusionment for man and woman is an accurate interpretation of this theme in
the poem. In his concluding statements, this critic states that Espronceda's association of love with the idea of Original Sin makes the artistic expression of the
figure of the devil unique in the poem: Luzbel is often teamed with God as equal
accomplices held responsible for the Edenic sin; however, the corruption of love
is solely attributed to the devil (229).

While this article is the first to treat the paradisiacal aspects of the Adamic
theme in *El diablo mundo*, it does not arrive at any conclusions regarding
Espronceda's Adamic hero, nor does the study treat the notion of evil beyond
the association of sin and "fallen" love. How are we to reconcile the notion of a
love that was somehow corrupted by Original Sin with the narrative segments
that portray Adán's exposure to the injustice of the world, his discovery of
death, and the indifference of God? The concept of love as paradise lost is essential to the understanding of the "Canto a Teresa," but does García Lorca's
model of corrupted love shed light on the meaning of the rest of the poem? The
notion of love as paradise is less obvious in the relationship between Salada and
Adán. The only example of this is evident when love between Salada and Adán
converts Salada's dingy room into a paradisiacal sanctuary: "la pobre estancia
con celeste encanto, / vertiendo en torno aromas de dulzura / que amor derrama
de su aéreo manto; / morada acaso triste, acaso impura, / mas de la dicha ahora
templo santo, / convertido en Edén de ricas flores / al soplo germinal de los
amores" (303). And love becomes impossible between Salada and Adán not
because of Adán's dream of finding a perfect love, but because of Adán's unfulfilled desire for riches and fame. He refuses Salada's unconditional love because
she cannot satisfy his material desires: ". . . Si me amas, si tu amor es cierto,
llévame al punto donde yo soñé . . . . / / Viento que en torno de mi frente
brame, / rayos que sienta sobre mí tronar, / triunfos, y glorias, y riquezas dame /
que derramen mis manos sin cesar" (335). Thus, regarding this pair of lovers,
Original Sin does not have the fatal effect that it is shown to have in the "Canto
a Teresa."

Stephen Vasari is another critic who has approached the poem within the framework of its myths. Vasari concludes that all the allusions to pagan and Christian myth in the work relate to the enigma of the nature of life and God. Calling the work a *"refundición"* of the first chapters of the Book of Genesis, Vasari interprets the poem allegorically as the human journey through life. Citing the example of Adán's first state of innocence and happiness, he relates it to the notion of paradise from the Genesis myth. Similarly, the unjustified imprisonment of Adán is viewed as an analogy to the Biblical myth, since the blameless character is incarcerated "sobre todo porque el patrón vive entre miedos constantes que alguien pudiera atentar contra su régimen o rebajar su autoridad" (181-82). Vasari goes on to state correctly that the poem is in opposition to the established religious and socio-political orders, and that it offers up its own myths "de una manera que parece sugerir que los mitos paganos valen tanto como la religión cristiana" (172). While he makes reference to many types of myth (classical, Biblical, gnostic, romantic), he fails to pursue with any concentrated effort the notion of the Old Testament myths in the work, nor even to consider fully the central meaning which he finds in the poem, the enigma of life and God.

Why does Espronceda choose to create an Adamic figure as the hero of his poem, and what is the relationship between the poem and the Biblical myths mentioned by Vasari? It seems that *El diablo mundo* bears a closer relation to the Adamic tradition than indicated by García Lorca's study of the "paradise" theme. Vasari's statement that Espronceda's poem is a "refundición" of the Genesis myths and that it offers its own myths that contradict the established myths is a correct interpretation of *El diablo mundo*, and is an area that deserves more attention, since Vasari did not pursue this avenue of thought.

The Adamic myth and the Combat myth had been repeated by previous literary artists for didactic and aesthetic reasons, but the Romantic's reading of the story would certainly have been unique. The liberal Romantic returns to the mythic beginnings because of his profound suspicion and doubt, or in the words of Casalduero, the Romantic doubt that is "un estado de ánimo—el estado en que se encuentra el hombre que no puede hallar la verdad" (*Forma y visión* 47). No longer able to accept the "truths" expounded by society, the artist sets out to attack and destroy the foundational myths that gave rise to the established belief system. In attacking the sacrosanct myths, the Romantic poet exercises his freedom in the rebellious act, discrediting the myth, so that he may assume the role of creator, freeing the imagination in order to create new myths in place of the old. The Romantic artist, notes Casalduero, may choose to ignore God, or if not, he can only remember God with feelings of pain and jealousy because "[e]l hombre romántico siente que Dios, con su omnipotencia, le quita el mundo; su autoridad absoluta no le deja gozar del mundo, ese mundo que el joven considera suyo, porque él lo crea, es la creación de su alma, de su yo, de su pura pasión" (*Espronceda* 237). Under the guise of total freedom of the individual, the Romantic artist must inevitably confront the Absolute, the idea of God, and the myths that sustain it, because these myths form the ideological basis, the history, that would limit the imagination and the creative impulse.

Doubt about the accepted truths and the inability to be subject to God causes the Romantic artist to possess a special attitude toward religion. Octavio Paz has written that all Romantics (liberal Romantics) believe in the notion of poetry as a substitute for religion: "los poetas son videntes y profetas, por su boca habla el espíritu. El poeta desaloja al sacerdote y la poesía se convierte en una revelación rival de la escritura religiosa" (75). This concept of the artist as prophet, as the interpretor, or creator, of inspired messages is vital to the reading of this Romantic verse, because the visions of Espronceda's Poet and old man, Pablo, represent a return to the old myths in order to question their validity, and ultimately, to destroy them. This idea is present in one of the unedited fragments of the poem where the Angel accuses the Poet of "negros pensamientos" and "loco desatino" because he dares to seek to comprehend the prohibited "arcano," the mysteries of life, evil, death, and even God:

> ¡Tú más alto, poeta, que los reyes,
> tú, cuyas santas leyes
> son las de tu conciencia y sentimiento;
> que a penetrar el pensamiento arcano
> osas alzar tu noble pensamiento,
> del mismo Dios, en tu delirio insano! (382)

The "arcano" is Espronceda's tree of the good and evil, his ancient symbol of forbidden knowledge, and Luzbel encourages the Poet to explore life's enigmas as he had tempted Eve to do:"¿Será en vano que tu mente / a otras esferas remontes, / sin que los negros arcanos / de vida y de muerte ahondes?" (184). Like Eve, the Poet is tempted to rebel against the ultimate taboo and to seek the truth, even if it means challenging the absolute authority of God. These are just two of the poem's many examples of the theme of the search for the ultimate truth, and in the poem Luzbel reveals his nature as temptor; nevertheless, in guiding the Poet in his fathoming of the enigmas of life, Luzbel becomes the angel of illumination, embodying the rational mind and the will to trespass all boundaries in order to conquer life's enigmas. In the figure of Luzbel, and in the audacious transgression committed by Eve in order to obtain knowledge of Good and Evil, Espronceda finds the rebel spirit he needs to challenge the ultimate authority. The rebel Poet as surrogate for the prophet leads directly to the idea of the poet as myth-maker, as the creator of the foundational stories that preserve the messages deemed important to the culture.

Cerny's conclusion that the discovery of evil is the main axis that gives meaning and coherence to this work will be the point of departure for the analysis of the Adamic myth and the Adamic figures in the poem, rather than the paradise theme and the association between love and Original Sin as expounded by García Lorca. Like the Adamic myth, *El diablo mundo* is a type of etion that seeks to explain or discover some aspect of human experience. Espronceda can not simply re-tell the story of the Adamic myth and the Combat myth, as did his mentor, Alberto Lista; but rather, he takes the liberty to construct his own "mythic" narration. Espronceda, using the remnants of Biblical myths, fabricates his own myths within the structure of his Poet's vision and Pablo's dream, taking the combat myth as his raw matter and creating in his Poet's inspired vision the pre-historical time of the liberation of the forces of evil into the world: ". . . que hoy su triste cárcel quiebran / libres los Diablos en fin, / y con música y estruendo / los condenados celebran, / juntos cantando y bebiendo, / un diabólico festín" (169). This nefarious vision, made up of the confusing array of sights and sounds that passes before the Poet in a moment, forms what the Poet calls the "breve compendio del mundo, / la tartárea bacanal" (174). Tartarus—the place in the Underworld reserved for those who had transgressed against god—combined with the Bacchanalia, the illicit excesses committed in the name of Bacchus, the giver of intoxicated joy, is a resonant metaphor here, suggesting the combination of illicit pleasure and condemnation that we find in the Adamic myth. In the Biblical myths of evil, the moment when Adam and Eve tasted the forbidden fruit was the fatal moment of the "Fall," when all the world changes. In Espronceda's myth, evil simply begins without any possible explanation. But there is other evidence pointing us to the Adamic myth.

In the Spanish literary recreations of the Adamic myth, the disruption of the harmony between the first humans and the elements of nature signaled that the bond between God and humanity had been breached, and that Adam and Eve's perfect state of innocence had been lost. As a punishment, death and evil are unleashed upon the world. In *El diablo mundo*, the Poet's vision also presents strange and sudden disruptions in the natural world as the evil beings advance, and here we find allusions to the beginning of death:

> Baladros lanzan y aullidos,
> silbos, relinchos, chirridos,
> y en desacordado estrépito,
> el fantástico escuadrón
> mueve horrenda algarabía
> con espantosa armonía,
> y horrísona confusión.

> Del toro ardiente al mugido
> responde en ronco graznar
> la malhadada corneja,
> y al agorero cantar
> de alguna hechicera vieja,
> el gato bufa y maúlla,
> el lobo erizado aúlla,
>      ladra furioso el mastín;
> y ruidos, voces y acentos
> mil se mezclan y confunden,
> y pavor y miedo infunden
> los bramidos de los vientos;
> que al mundo amagan su fin
> en guerra los elementos. (171)

Not only do the natural elements foretell the demonic liberation, but death accompanies evil and the apocalyptic end of humanity is repeated by the elements and by martial images: "Allí bramidos de guerra / se escuchan, y el golpear / del acero, y de las trompas / el estrépito marcial, / aquí relinchar caballos / y estruendo de pelear; / allí retumban cañones, / lamentos suenan allá / y alaridos, voces, ayes / y súplicas y llorar" (173). The entrance or liberation of evil, the strange disruption in the natural world, the apocalyptic nature of the vision, and the metaphor of the world as a "tartárea bacanal" all point to the Adamic myth and the introduction of evil at the decisive moment of the Fall. The introduction of Luzbel and his rebel band into the vision alludes directly to the combat myth and, by association, to the Eden narration where the serpent tempts Eve. The vision seems to be composed of remnants, images, and allusions to the Adamic myth and the combat myth. So in the beginning of his poem, Espronceda establishes a relationship between the ancient myths and his poem, thus raising the metaphysical questions of the nature of good and evil, life and death, that the Biblical cosmogonies expressed in the metaphorical triangle of God, humanity, and Satan.

Given that the first vision focuses on the figure of Luzbel and the combat motif, it continues the apocalyptic design of the Christian epic poems on lost innocence by Milton and his Spanish followers. But Espronceda adds a decisively modern twist. Unlike the dramatists and the poets who have treated the Adamic myth by placing the characters and incidents in a cosmic setting where Heaven, Hell, and the Earth converge, Espronceda gives the conflict a new locus—now the battleground is centered within the imagination of the Poet. Espronceda's Satan, who first appears in the vision in his customary form: an "infernal gigante" of "negra figura / de colosal estatura / y de imponente ademán," with serpents for hair (178), reveals his true nature to the Poet, and, in doing so, manages an interesting turn in the Biblical construction of the figure. Luzbel appears, and begins to raise a series of questions about the nature of God, humanity, and his own nature. Eventually, he confesses his true origin:

> Tú me engendraste, mortal,
> y hasta me diste un nombre;
> pusiste en mí tus tormentos,
> en mi alma tus rencores,
> en mi mente tu ansiedad,
> en mi pecho tus furores,
> en mi labio tus blasfemias
> e impotentes maldiciones;
> me erigiste en tu verdugo,
> me tributaste temores,
> y entre Dios y yo partiste
> el imperio de los orbes.
> Y yo soy parte de ti,
> soy ese espírtu insomne
> que te excita y te levanta
> de tu nada a otras regiones,
> con pensamiento de ángel,
> con mezquindades de hombre. (183)

So within the Poet's vision, composed mostly of images of the turbulent forces of nature, battle cries, and images of human destruction, Espronceda's Poet experiences first the presence of a vague, unspecified evil, the "nuevo Luzbel" that reveals itself to be none other than man's own nature. Having declared his human origin, the figure transfers onto the Poet his spirit of daring rebellion, further justifying the challenge to the established law. Luzbel confesses to the Poet: "Acaso yo soy / el espíritu del hombre, / . . . [que] osa apartar los rayos / que a Dios misterioso esconden, / y analizarle atrevido / frente a frente se propone" (182). The link between the diabolical figure and humanity is made evident again when Luzbel recounts that he is "el ángel de los dolores, / el rey del mal, y mi infierno / es el corazón del hombre" (185). In his unique version of the combat myth, Espronceda centers Luzbel and the idea of evil in the recesses of the human spirit, thus destroying the Christian notion of the figure as a separate, radical instigator of human evil.

Having discredited the notion of Luzbel as a separate "cosmic" entity responsible for humanity's plight, Espronceda proceeds to question the validity of other Christian ideas. If Luzbel the temptor urges the Poet to investigate the "arcano" of life's mysteries, Luzbel, the enemy of God, becomes a structural device through which Espronceda attacks the established myths and ideas of Christianity. In the figure's sardonic interrogative about the nature of God, Espronceda gives voice to his anger at the ineffectual Christian myths, and he ridicules the notion of a world governed by a "benevolent" and "just" God:

> ¿Es Dios tal vez el Dios de la venganza,
> y hierve el rayo en su irritada mano,
> y la angustia, el dolor, la muerte lanza
> al inocente que le implora en vano?
> ¿Es Dios el Dios que arranca la esperanza,
> frívolo, injusto y sin piedad tirano,
> del corazón del hombre, y le encadena,
> y a eterna muerte al pecador condena?
>
> Embebido en su inmenso poderío,
> ¿Es Dios el Dios que goza en su hermosura,
> que arrojó el universo en el vacío,
> leyes le dio y abandonó su hechura?
> ¿Fue vanidad del hombre y desvarío
> soñarse imagen de su imagen pura?

¿Es Dios el Dios que en su eternal sosiego

ni vio su llanto ni escuchó su ruego? (181)

The series of strophes brings into question the nature of God, and indirectly portrays the Almighty as a frivolous, angry, vain, unjust, and indifferent being. Although the words come from Luzbel, this audacious attack on God's character reflects the ultimate rebel spirit of the Romantic, who cannot find any consolation in the existing myths that his culture values, and so in questioning the myths, he plants the seeds for their destruction. Espronceda's indictment of the Old Testament God culminates in the scene that Cerny described as a Hugoesque antithesis: the scene where Adán confronts the mourning woman and innocently suggests that God will answer her prayer to bring her daughter back to life. The contrast between Adán's candid innocence about the nature of God and the old woman's staunch faith in light of her tragedy point out the absurdity of believing in an uncaring, absent God. As the mother speaks to her dead daughter, she attempts to justify the death by means of her belief: "El Señor me la dio y él me la quita" and "Dios te llevó consigo; / mas es dura mi pena, / y cruel, aunque justo, mi castigo." Meanwhile, Adán tries to learn more about this strange God: "El Dios ese que habita, / omnipotente en la región del cielo, / ¿quién es que inunda a veces de alegría, / y otras veces cruel con mano impía, / llena de angustia y de dolor el suelo?" (373-374). These depictions of God as indifferent to the suffering of the mother ennoble the innocence of humanity and represent nothing less than an attack on the Christian scheme of Salvation, for there is no indication of any Redemption in the vision nor in the poem. Luzbel's interrogation about life leads ultimately to the suggestion that the God of the Old Testament does not exist; on the contrary, a unique and secret power might be the origin of life: ¿Tal vez secreto espíritu del mundo / el universo anima y alimenta, / y derramado su hálito fecundo / alborota la mar y el cielo argenta, / y a cuanto el orbe en su ámbito profundo / tímido esconde o vanidoso ostenta, / presta con su virtud desconocida / alma, razón, entendimiento y vida? (181). This secret spirit of the world becomes the creative force in Pablo's vision, and a central figure in Espronceda's myth of the Creation.

If the Poet's vision was informed by elements and images of the combat myth that serve to attack the notions of absolute good and evil, Espronceda's portrayal of the creation of Adán presents an interesting combination of incidents that allude to the Genesis A and B cosmogonies. Having raised questions about the existence of God of the Old Testament, the creation of Adán occurs under the guidance of an omnipotent, mysterious energy, the seminal power of life that creates a new man out of the old Pablo. This energy or life force is first expressed in a group of contrasting images of birth, death, destruction, and perpetuity as an angelic voice welcomes the enigmatic being: "Salve, llama creadora del mundo, / lengua ardiente de eterno saber, / puro germen, principio fecundo / que encadenas la muerte a tus pies" (206). The new deity is the "fuerza secreto del mundo," the energy that moves the universe. The power of the sun, the moon, the elements, colors, sounds, and scents are touched by this mysterious, feminine, essence of life. As a Creatress, this being resembles the Gods of the Genesis cosmologies. Like the artisan God of Genesis B, she works her material into forms, and like the distant God of Genesis A, she commands life into existence: "Tú la inerte materia espoleas, / tú la ordenas juntarse y vivir, / tú su lodo modelas y creas / miles seres de formas sin fin" (206).

With his unique creation myth, Espronceda has moved beyond the Biblical cosmogonies to a more primal power than that of Jahweh, or of the God of Genesis A. Espronceda recurs to the feminine creative force of the Earth Mother that the Patriarchs sought to suppress with their myths. The poet later calls this omnipotent creator the "deidad" and the "diosa encantadora," and she nurtures the feeble Pablo, who is in the throes of death, with the fecund energy of her creative seed: "De la vida en el hondo océano / flota el hombre en perpetuo vaivén, / y derrama abundante tu mano / la creadora semilla en su ser" (208). While the creation myths of the Genesis portray death as a punishment for disobedience, casting it as a force in opposition to the creation, Espronceda's Goddess encompasses death as the agent that releases primal matter, allowing it to be reshaped: "Desbarata tus obras en vano / vencedora la muerte tal vez, / de sus restos levanta tu mano / nuevas obras triunfante otra vez" (206). In his dream, as Pablo lies enveloped by death, he is commanded to taste the "eterno raudal" of this primal life force in order attain his new, immortal life. Thus, Adám is created anew out of the process of Pablo's death, like the Mesopotamian myth of creation where the slain dragon, Tiamat, becomes the primordial soup of the heavens, the earth, and all living creatures.

While the Adamic myth and the Combat myth serve Espronceda as the raw material with which to attack the staid notions of good and evil, they also serve the poet as remnants with which to create his own mythic narration that seeks to fulfill the etiological function of the Adamic and the Combat myths, which was to explain the origin of evil. Eve's quest for knowledge and wisdom, her audacity, and her transgression of God's authority, and Luzbel's guidance of the humans and his enmity with God are the spiritual models for Espronceda's poem.

Luzbel and Eve become symbols for the restless rebel spirit in humanity, providing a human justification to question, challenge, and even attack the Biblical myths that formed the basis of the Christian scheme of Salvation. If the Combat myth was used to discredit the cosmological figure of Luzbel, and to attack the idea of God, thus refuting the notion of a radical non-human beginning of evil, the Adamic character in the poem serves to point to humanity as the victim of life's or God's circumstances. Adán is not a rejuvenated man who has bargained his youth as was Faust, nor is he a man reared by animals like Andrenio. The character is portrayed as a new man, that is, a man without memory of his previous existence, a man unjaded by bitter experiences, and with a mind full of dreams: ". . . y el alma y todo nuevo, / todo esperanzas el feliz mancebo" (242). The emphasis on the candid nature of Adán forms the basis with which Espronceda contrasts innocence and cruelty, dreams and disillusionments of life. Adán is the opposite of the poet of the "Canto a Teresa," the disillusioned man who had set love as his ideal, only to have his world shattered by death, and thus, the character's candidness towards life contrasts with Espronceda's cynicism. But Adán is also the opposite of God, for Espronceda's hero proves that he genuinely cares for the old woman's plight, while it is made obvious that God does not. There is no doubt as to the purity of Adán's soul even though he is adept in the skills of the criminal:

> Ni leyes sabe, ni conoce el mundo,
> sólo a su instinto generoso atiende,
> y un abismo de crímenes inmundo
> cruza y el crimen por virtud aprende.
> Y aquel pecho que es noble sin segundo
> y que el valor y el entusiasmo enciende,
> aplica al crimen la virtud que alienta
> y puro es si criminal se ostenta. (285)

Espronceda's Adam is the image of the sublime criminal, whose heart is noble, and whose criminal actions are mitigated by the fact that the figure's criminality is the result of circumstance. The evil that befalls Adán serves to indict humanity and to incriminate God by suggesting that humanity is not the victim of a separate evil, but the victim of the unjust laws of society and of the universe. Cerny is correct in stating that Espronceda does not arrive at any definite conclusions as to the nature of evil; nevertheless, having discredited the figure of Satan as a separate origin of human evil, and given the numerous attacks against

God, Espronceda seems to suggest that if there were a supreme deity like the Christian model, then that deity would have to be held responsible for evil, suffering, and injustice in the world. Perhaps by bringing into question the Biblical myths of the beginning of evil, Espronceda is suggesting that evil may be defined as the absence of absolute good, or the absence of the Christian God. These questions cannot be answered completely. However, Espronceda's use of the Adamic myth and his depiction of Adán as sublime criminal manage to invalidate the notion of Original Sin since the primal paradisiacal state is made impossible by the destruction of the Biblical myths.

# Conclusion

In this study, I have set forth the characteristics of what I labeled the Spanish Adamic tradition. Given that the origin of all the dramatic and poetic texts created by the peninsular authors is the mytho-poetic narrative that dates to the earliest writings of the Torah, and may have existed in the oral cultures of the Near East, further investigation of the incidents and figures of the narration known as the Genesis B cosmogony have emphasized the narrative complexity of a seemingly simple story. While the Adamic story is familiar to most people in the West, it is not generally known that the facile, albeit puzzling, narration, is an amalgamation of elements from earlier mythic traditions. Rather than functioning as a cosmogony, the Adamic story proves to be the result of the intentional intervention of Priestly editors who molded the tale into a form that would express the meanings that appeared to answer their foundational questions about humanity, nature, and God. I have pointed out the relationship between the Biblical narrative and the non-Biblical notions of the beginning of evil, Eden as Paradise, Original Sin, and the metaphor of the Fall, all of which may have originated in the centuries of exegetical writings concentrating on the myth. As a foundational narrative in the Judeo-Christian tradition, Adam was believed the historical genesis of humanity, the beginning of historical or linear time, and thus, the figure became a prototype for all humans. The writings of Paul related the figure of Adam to the "second Adam," and consequently demytholgized the figure, lending a historical veracity to the tale and its characters.

Throughout this study I have used the term "myth" loosely to refer to the Biblical narrative of Adam and Eve, as well as to the associated themes and skeletal narratives which are related to the Adamic figure and its texts. Borrowing theories from myth criticism, I have adopted as a central hypothesis the idea that no literary work is formed in a vacuum; therefore, even the most basic narrative will yield its cultural riches when placed within the historical and cultural environments that may have informed the text. It is also the premise of this study that a myth is generally considered a culturally important narrative, since it is believed that these narratives express the foundational messages deemed necessary for cultural survival. Thus, I have proceeded to show a relationship between the importance of the Adamic myth as a didactic tool of the Counter-Reformation and its depiction in dramatic form, where the manner of depicting the characters and incidents of the myth reflected to some extent the meaning of the dramatic pieces.

The story of Adam and Eve may have captured the attention of the Renaissance because of a renewed interest in the history of humanity, but as an essential episode in the Christian History of Salvation, the Adamic story and its figure were reduced to basic cultural signs that were deemed fundamental to the ideological welfare of the Church. Therefore, it was necessary that the Adamic narrative be made readily accessible to all of society, especially to the marginalized and rural segments where religious practices were less established. With Luther's challenge to the ideological basis of the Church, the story was promoted as a tool of propaganda emphasizing the role of free will in the course of human salvation. Writers of the *autos* in the sixteenth and seventeenth centuries composed dramatic works that served to propagate the Church's message of humanity's evil transgression and the need for priestly intervention in the process of salvation since Original Sin and free will were the central themes of these pieces. Here the Adamic myth was reduced to a few elements needed to portray Adam and Eve as symbols of the ruptured relationship between humanity, God, and nature. Lope de Vega depicted his version of the story in three acts by including the story of Cain and Abel, and his interpretation reflects his proclivity for making the utmost out of the dramatic possibilities in the story. His *La creación del mundo y primera culpa de nuestro padre Adán* portrays Adam as a passionate husband, willing to sacrifice his life and his relationship with God for the love of Eve. Yet, the character is shown to be the wise and repentant father who regrets the evil consequences of his deed when he sees them perpetuated in his son, Cain. While the *autos* tended to portray Adam as a type, Lope developed the mythic figure into a dramatic character.

If the sixteenth and early seventeenth-century writers had based their dramatic texts of the Fall of man on the Book of Genesis, the principal locus of the story for writers during the later eighteenth century was to be found in Milton's epic *Paradise Lost*. Here, the aesthetic ideals of the Seville school became the impetus for the subsequent literary portrayals of the Adamic myth after the Spanish discovery of Milton's epic. It seems the notion of imitation of classical models, and the idea of the epic as the most cherished genre became central to the ruling Neo-classicist aesthetic that inspired attempts by Lista and Reinoso to create a Spanish religious epic that might rival the English poem. When compared to their model, the belated attempts by the Seville poets were inferior to *Paradise Lost*, but their efforts are important to this study, in that the two poems entitled *La inocencia perdida* represent a continuation of the literary representation of the Adamic myth in Spain, forming a direct line leading to the nation's most important Romantic poem, *El diablo mundo*. Not only did Lista and Reinoso include the draconic figure and the myth of the "fallen" angels as a central part of their retelling of the story, but their anthropomorphic depictions of the Almighty may have inspired (at least in part) Espronceda's bitter attacks against the God of the Old Testament.

*EL diablo mundo* bears a closer relationship to the Adamic myth than García Lorca, Cerny, and Vasari have indicated. While preliminary readings of Espronceda's poem and Gracián's *El Criticón* show many similarities regarding the uses of the characters of Adán and Andrenio, further investigation reveals that Gracián and Espronceda were quite opposite in their literary depictions of the figure of Adam. Unlike Gracián, who seems to have played down the association of Andrenio with Adam, Espronceda not only borrows remnants from the Adamic myth and the Combat myth, but he uses the figures of Lucifer, Eve, and Adam as the spiritual models for the literary depiction of his liberal rebellion. Taking as a point of departure the suppositions or traditional meanings that the Combat myth and the Adamic myths entail, Espronceda took the liberty to "re-create" the Genesis stories in a new form, like fragments of different objects assembled into a new whole. It seems that this liberal Romantic understood well the ambivalence and irrationality of the myths on which Christianity had based its ideology, and he used elements of the Biblical myths as a means to discredit the cultural meaning that they put forth.

Thus, in Espronceda's poem we find fragments that make the narrative appear irrational, and the poem possesses a numinous quality that is also found in the Biblical Genesis. Here Espronceda places his own myths within the visionary plane as if to re-create the sacrosanct realm with which the Biblical myths are generally held. The vision of the Poet and the vision of Pablo present new examples of the Combat myth and the Creation myth that function as a means to subvert the Biblical stories from which they are drawn. In Espronceda's portrayal of the Adamic figure, Adam becomes simultaneously the pure innocent and adept criminal, thus, destroying the ideas of Original Sin and Lucifer as a radical origin of evil. The inclination towards malefaction is shown to be part of human nature, and thus, humanity is shown to be no more culpable than God who remains aloof to suffering, death, and injustice.

Given that *El diablo mundo* highlights the subversive nature of the mythic figures it borrows from the Bible, it expresses the anger of the liberal Romantic against the established religious order; and given that the poem was deemed the most important one in Castilian at the time of its publication, it is likely that it would have come to the attention of one Victor Rosselló, whose *La caída de Adán* should be linked to the likes of Fernán Caballero and Alarcón, because it represents a reaction to Romantic art. Rosselló produced an overt criticism of the lost sense of direction that the true Romantics expressed. This may explain Rosselló's insistence on the veracity of the Biblical story and the denunciation of those men of science who would deny the existence of God. As Donald Shaw has noted regarding the anti-Romantic reaction in Spain, this was literature wholly against the exaltation of desperation and pain of the individual and in support of a literary expression that proved "útil a la familia y a la sociedad . . . , consolador del espíritu humano," (248-49). This would explain Rosselló's "faithful" realistic rendition of the Biblical story and his proselytizing attitude in the poem.

What to make of a culturally significant myth that has been informed by more than fifteen centuries of speculative writings, and whose content has been amplified and reduced by the works of theologians, dramatists, poets, and graphic artists? When we consider the history of the Adamic myth, we find that because the cultural data of the myth did not lose its relevancy to society, it continued to remain viable. Continuation means that metamorphosis is inevitable, because the creation and dissemination of the nexus of symbolic values pertaining to the Adamic figure and myth were only possible as a consequence of dynamic processes of repetition. The Adamic theme remained viable and was repeated because it was somehow made meaningful to each successive generation that encountered it. And so, the function of the myth changed from a wholly theological one in the *autos* and the *comedias*, to a predominantly aesthetic one in the *canto épico*. Espronceda's poem utilized the myth for aesthetic reasons, in order to destroy the theological function. Finally, Rosselló's anti-Romantic expression proved to be an attempt to infuse the religious or theological function into the myth that had been rendered ineffectual by *El diablo mundo*.

The cultural importance of the Genesis A and B cosmogonies assured intense scrutiny by intellectuals and artistic repetitions of the narrations by theologians and artists. New versions in new media inspired further repetitions. It might be said that the story of Adam and Eve has engendered multitudes of repetitions of the "original" model. The central problem of the meaning of a myth is one of the relation of a sign to its referent within an unstable cultural environment. In his book *Simulations*, Jean Baudrillard has written that the proliferation of signs attesting to a certain meaning may result in a distortion and loss of the meaning. More specifically, with regards to religious signs, Baudrillard notes that icons tend to destroy the divine entity for which they are a testament. Thus, a deity is reduced to the "signs that attest his existence" and the whole system of "God" signs becomes a "giant simulacrum, not unreal, but a simulacrum, never again exchanging for what is real, but exchanging in itself, in an uninterrupted circuit without reference or circumference" (10-11). The result: a "Hades of simulation, which is no longer one of torture, but of subtle, maleficent, elusive twisting of meaning" (34). The Spanish versions of the Adamic myth serve as visible artifacts that attest to such an evolution (destruction) of meaning of foundational texts in society, and also as a meeting ground between the ancient and the contemporary worlds. It should not surprise us that this myth continues to be revitalized in Christian societies as the human need to understand the malevolent aspect of our existence does not diminish with each new generation.

# Endnotes

## Chapter 1

[1]Quotation from Elaine Pagel's reproduction of the first three chapters of Genesis (Revised Standard Version) in *Adam, Eve, and the Serpent*, p. xi.

[2]Understandably, the translations of the text have failed to render the humor that Rosenberg and Bloom have found in the Hebrew version. Rosenberg's *The Book of J* is a new translation of the Jahwist text whose purpose is to rediscover the "original" text that he feels has been lost to the sententious language of the Biblical scholars.

[3]Rosenberg's translation.

[4]First three chapters of Genesis reproduced from the *Biblia castellana of 1420* and quoted in the introduction to Lope de Vega's "La creación del mundo y primera culpa del hombre" in *Obras de Lope de Vega: Autos y coloquios*, p. xxvii.

[5]The absence of the Fall has been pointed out by Claus Westermann, *Creation*, (Philadelphia: Fortress Press, 1974) p. 108—109; and by F.R. Tennant, *The Origin and Propagation of Sin*, (Cambridge: University Press, 1906).

[6]Elaine Pagels' *Adam, Eve and the Serpent*, (1989) deals with the myth in the first centuries of Christianity when it may have signified freedom as well as other notions to early Christians.

[7]In the second century Iraenaeus, Tatian, Theophilus of Antioch, Clement of Alexandria, and Chrysostom presented systems of exegesis that contested these writings. Irenaeus in *The Detection and Overthrow of the False Gnosis* presented his interpretation of a childlike Adam, cast in the physical and moral image of God. The view of Adam as infant does not preclude the idea of Original Sin. Whether Adam was saved or not was proposed by Tatian in *Orations to the Greeks*, and this question initiated a topic of debate that would last for a thousand years. The effect of Adam's transgression on his descendants was proposed by Theophilus who believed that free will was the determining

factor in the mortality or immortality of Adam's descendants. Clement and the Greeks Athanasius, Chrysostom, and Gregory of Nazianzus were in agreement with this view (York 109).

# Chapter 2

[1]Du Bartas's *Seconde semaine* (1584), Hugo Grotius's *Adamus Exul* (1601), Andreini's *L'Adamo* (1613), Francesco Loredan's *La scena tragica d'Adamo e Eva* (1644), Serafino della Salandra's *Adamo caduto* (1647), Samuel Pordage's *Mudorum explicatio* (1661), Jost Van den Vondel's *Adam banni* (1664), and John Milton's *Paradise Lost* (1674) are some of the most noted non-Spanish works during these two centuries.

[2]Wardropper agrees with A. A. Parker that the central theme, or the asunto, of the auto sacramental is the Eucharist (36). Pérez Priego also considers this sacrament as the point of convergence for all the plays in the *Código* (37). Dietz has argued that the focus in the auto is not the Eucharist per se, but, like the English cycle, the main theme is the entire history of God's involvement in human affairs (77).

[3]Two plays, the *Aucto del peccado de Adán* and the *Auto de los hierros de Adán* were published in Rouanet's *Colección de autos, farsas y coloquios del siglo XVI*. The *Aucto de la prevaricación de nuestro padre Adán* and the *Farsa del sacramento de Adán* were taken from Pérez Priego's *Códice de autos viejos*. The majority of the plays are belived to have been written between 1550 and 1578 according to Pérez Priego's data. For the purposes of this study, the general chronological frame is all that matters.

[4]The *Farsa del triunfo del sacramento* names Estado de Inocencia and Pecado Original as two of its characters. In *La justicia contra el pecado de Adán*, Hombre is defended by Angel de la Guarda from the accusations of Justicia and Misericordia. The *Auto de acusación contra el género humano*, the *Farsa racional del Libre Albedrío* and *El árbol de la vida* by Valdivieso all deal with moral and spiritual conflicts of the human condition. See *La alegoría en los autos y farsas anteriores a Calderón* by Louise Fothergill-Payne.

[5]In *The Ideas of the Fall*, N. P. Williams points out the vagueness of the Council's language on related issues of the notion of the pre-lapsarian and post-lapsarian states of Adam, including the Fall and Original Sin (419-423).

[6]Emphasis is mine, here illustrating Eve's language of persuasion.

[7]There are two instances where the voice of God is heard on stage. The first is an acknowledgment that God has accepted Abel's offering: "Abel, Dios ha recibido / tu amoroso ofrecimiento, / Y á sus oídos llegaron / Tus clamores y tus ruegos" (187). The second example occurs after Abel's death when the voice of God asks Cain: where is your brother? (188).

## Chapter 3

[1]It is uncertain whether the poem by Valderrábano, "La caída de Luzbel," and a similar poem on the subject by Donato Arenzana and cited by Lasso de la Vega (30) are extant.

[2]Quintana published his critique of the poem, "Juicio del Poema 'La incencia perdida,'" in Variedades de Ciencias, Literatura y Artes 1804, Tomo III, pp. 356-363. The date of Blanco's response in the same periodical is unknown.

## Chapter 4

[1]"Las posibles fuentes literarias de Espronceda en El diablo mundo" in *Boletín de la Biblioteca Menéndez Pelayo*. 45 (1969), 271-325.

# Works Cited

Alborg, Juan Luis. *Historia de la literatura española: siglo XVIII*. Madrid: Gredos, 1972.

Alvarez-Buylla, José Benito. "La traducción de Jovellanos del libro primero de *Paraíso Perdido* de Milton." *Filología moderna*, 10 (1963): 1-47.

Arias, Ricardo. *The Spanish Sacramental Plays*. Boston: Twayne, 1980.

Armstrong, John H.S. *The Paradise Myth*. London: Oxford UP, 1969.

Armstrong, Karen. *A History of God*. New York: Ballantine, 1993.

Baudrillard, Jean. *Simulations*. New York: Columbia UP, 1983.

Bergmann, Martin S. *The Anatomy of Loving: The Story of Man's Quest to Know What Love Is*. New York: Fawcett Columbine, 1991.

Beverley, John R. "On the Concept of the Spanish Literary Baroque." *Culture and Control in Counter-Reformation Spain*. Eds. Anne J. Cruz and Mary Elizabeth Perry. Minneapolis: U of Minneapolis P, 1992.

Bloom, Harold. *The Anxiety of Influence*. Oxford: Oxford UP, 1973.

____. *Ruin the Sacred Truths: Poetry and Belief from the Bible to the Present*. Cambridge: Harvard UP, 1991.

Bonilla y San Martín, Adolfo. "El pensamiento de Espronceda." *La España moderna*. 234 (1908) 69-101.

"Book of Genesis." *Encyclopaedia Judaica*, 1971 ed.

Bretz, Mary Lee. "*El diablo mundo* y sus relaciones con la literatura europea moderna." *Arbor* 403-04 (1979): 87-94.

Campbell, Joseph. *The Masks of God: Occidental Mythology*. New York: Penguin, 1964.

Casalduero, Joaquín. *Espronceda*. Madrid: Gredos, 1967.

_____. *Forma y visión de* El diablo mundo *de Espronceda*. Madrid: Insula, 1951.

Cassirer, Ernst. *The Individual and the Cosmos in Renaissance Philosophy*. New York: Barnes and Noble, 1963.

Castro, Américo. "Acerca de *El diablo mundo* de Espronceda." *Revista de Filología Española* 7 (1920): 274-378.

Cerny, Vaclav. "Quelques remarques sur les sentiments religieux chez Rivas et Espronceda." *Bulletin Hispanique* 36 (1934): 71-87.

Colford, William E. *Juan Meléndez Valdés: A Study in the Transition from Neo-Classicism to Romanticism in Spanish Poetry*. New York: Hispanic Institute, 1942.

Cuddon, J. A. "Fable." *A Dictionary of Literary Terms*. New York: Doubleday, 1980.

Dedieu, Jean Pierre. "'Christianization' in New Castile: Catechism, Communion, Mass, and Confirmation in the Toledo Archbishopric, 1540-1650." *Culture and Control in Counter-Reformation Spain*. Eds. Anne J. Cruz and Mary Elizabeth Perry. Minneapolis: U of Minnesota P, 1992.

Del Río, Angel. *Historia de la literatura española: Desde 1700 hasta nuestros días*. New York: Dryden, 1985.

Delumeau, Jean. *Sin and Fear: The Emergence of a Western Guilt Culture, 13th-18th Centuries*. New York: St. Martin's P, 1990.

Demerson, Georges. *Don Juan Meléndez Valdés y su tiempo*. Madrid: Taurus, 1971.

Dietz, Donald T. "Liturgical and Allegorical Drama: The Uniqueness of Calderón's *Auto Sacramental*." *Calderón de la Barca at the Tercentenary*. Eds.

Wendell Aycock and Sydney P. Cravens. Lubbock: Texas Tech U, 1982. 71-88.

Díez Borque, José María. "Notas sobre la crítica para un estudio del personaje de la comedia española del siglo de oro." *Teoría del personaje.* Ed. Carlos Castilla del Pino. Madrid: Alianza, 1989.

Donovan, Richard B. *Liturgical Drama in Medieval Spain.* Toronto: Pontifical Institute of Medieval Studies, 1958.

Doty, William G. *Mythography: The Study of Myths and Rituals.* Tuscaloosa: U of Alabama P, 1986.

Duarte, Julio M. "Estudio y edición crítica de *La creación del mundo y primera culpa del hombre*." Diss. Emory U, 1968.

Elliot, J. H. *Imperial Spain: 1469-1716.* London: Penguin, 1990.

Espronceda, José de. *El estudiante de Salamanca; El diablo mundo.* Madrid: Castalia, 1987.

Evans, J.M. Paradise Lost *and the Genesis Tradition.* London: Oxford UP, 1968.

Flecniakoska, Jean-Louis. "Les conflits tragiques dans l'auto religieux précaldéronien." *Theátre tragique.* Ed. J. Jacquot. Paris: Editions du Centre National de la Recherche Scientifique, 1962: 107-117.

Flecniakoska, Jean-Louis. "Les rôles de Satan dans les pieces du Códice de Autos Viejos." *Revue des Langues Romances* 75 (1963): 195-207.

Forsyth, Neil. *The Old Enemy: Satan and the Combat Myth.* Princeton: Princeton UP, 1987.

Fothergill-Payne, Louise. *La alegoría en los autos y farsas anteriores a Calderón.* London: Tamesis, 1977.

Frazer, James George. *Folk-lore in the Old Testament: Studies in Comparative Religion, Legend and Law.* London: Macmillan, 1919.

Freilich, Morris. "Myth, Method, and Madness." *Current Anthropology*. 16.2 (1975): 207-26.

García Lorca, Francisco. *De Garcilaso a Lorca*. Madrid: Istmo, 1984.

Ginzberg, Louis. *The Legends of the Jews*. 7 vols. Philadelphia: n.p., 1913-38.

Glaser, Edward. "Lope de Vega's *La creación del mundo y primera culpa del hombre*." *Annali del' Istituto Orientale di Napoli*. Naples: Sezione Germanica, 1962. 29-56.

Glendinning, Nigel. "Influencia de la literatura inglesa en el siglo XVIII." *Cuadernos de la Cátedra Feijoo*. 22 (1970): 47-94.

González, Gabriel. *Drama y teología en el siglo de oro*. Salamanca: Ediciones Universidad de Salamanca, 1987.

Gracián, Baltasar. *El Criticón*. Madrid: Cátedra, 1984.

Graves, Robert and Raphael Patai. *Hebrew Myths: The Book of Genesis*. London: Cassell, 1964.

Graves, Robert. *Adam's Rib and Other Anomalous Elements in the Hebrew Creation Myth*. London: Trianon, 1955.

Green, Otis H. *The Literary Mind of Medieval and Renaissance Spain*. Lexington: U of Kentucky, 1970.

Griffin, Dustin. "Milton's Literary Influence." *The Cambridge Companion to Milton*. Ed. Dennis Danielson. Cambridge: Cambridge UP, 1989.

Hainsworth, J. B. *The Idea of Epic*. Berkeley: U of California P, 1991.

Hazard, Paul. *El pensamiento europeo en el siglo XVIII*. Madrid: Alianza Universidad, 1985.

Heinberg, Richard. *Memories and Visions of Paradise: Exploring the Universal Myth of a Lost Golden Age*. Los Angeles: Jeremy P. Tarcher, 1989.

Howatson, M.C. ed. *The Oxford Companion to Classical Literature*. Oxford: Oxford UP, 1989.

Hughes, Merritt Y. Introduction. *Paradise Lost*. By John Milton. Indianapolis: Odyssey, 1979.

Huizinga, J. *The Waning of the Middle Ages*. Garden City: Doubleday Anchor, 1954.

Hunter, G. K. *Paradise Lost*. London: Allen and Unwin, 1980.

Juretschke, Hans. *Vida, obra y pensamiento de Alberto Lista*. Madrid: Escuela de Historia Moderna, 1951.

Kamen, Henry. *Inquisition and Society in Spain*. Bloomington: Indiana UP, 1985.

Kassier, Theodore L. *The Truth Disguised: Allegorical Structure and Technique in Gracián's 'Criticón'*. London: Tamesis, 1976.

Kerenyi, C. *Prometheus: Archetypal Image of Human Experience*. New York: Pantheon, 1963.

Kirkconnell, Watson. *The Celestial Cycle: The Theme of Paradise Lost in World Literature*. Toronto: U of Toronto P, 1952

Lasso de la Vega y Argüelles, Angel. *Historia y juicio crítico de la escuela poética sevillana*. Madrid: Manuel Tello, 1876.

Lázaro Carreter, Fernando. *Teatro medieval*. Madrid: Castalia, 1976.

Lefkovitz, Lori Hope. "Creating the World: Structuralism and Semiotics." *Contemporary Literary Theory*. Eds. G. Douglas Atkins and Laura Morrow, Amherst: U of Massachusetts P, 1989.

Lerner, Gerda. *The Creation of Patriarchy*. Oxford: Oxford UP, 1986.

Levin, Harry. *The Myth of the Golden Age in the Renaissance*. Bloomington, 1969.

Lista, Alberto. "De la moderna escuela sevillana de literatura." *Revista de Madrid.* 1.1 (1838): 251-276.

_____. "La inocencia perdida." *Poemas épicos.* Ed. Cayetano Rosell. Madrid: Biblioteca de Autores Españoles, 1864. 503-507.

Lopéz Estrada, F. *Tomás Moro y España,* Madrid: 1980.

Lovejoy, Arthur O. and Boas George. *Primitivism and Related Ideas in Antiquity.* Baltimore: 1935.

Luzán, Ignacio de. *La poética o reglas de la poesía en general y de sus principales especies.* Barcelona: Labor, 1977.

MacCaffrey, Isabel Gamble. *Paradise Lost as "Myth".* Cambridge: Harvard UP, 1959.

Maravall, J. A. *Estudios de historia del pensamiento español.* Madrid: Ediciones Cultura Hispánica, 1984.

Marrast, Robert. *Espronceda y su tiempo.* Barcelona: Editorial Crítica, 1989.

_____. Introduction. *El diablo mundo.* By Espronceda. Madrid: Castalia, 1987.

Martinengo, Alessandro. *Polimorfismo nel 'Diablo mundo' d'Espronceda.* Turin: Buttega d'Erasmo, 1962.

Mazzei, Pilade. *La poesia de Espronceda.* Firenze: La Nuova Italia, 1935.

McDannell, Colleen and Bernhard Lang. *Heaven: A History.* New York: Vintage, 1988.

Meléndez Valdés, Juan. *Obras en verso.* Oviedo: Cátedra Feijoo, 1983.

Metford, J.C.J. "Alberto Lista and the Romantic Movement in Spain." *Liverpool Studies in Spanish Literature. First Series: From Cadalso to Rubén Darío.* Ed. E. Allison Peers. Liverpool: Institute of Hispanic Studies, 1940. 19-43.

Milton, John. *Paradise Lost*. ed Merritt Y. Hughes. Indianapolis: Odyssey, 1962.

Moreno Villa, José. "Prologue" to *El diablo mundo*. Madrid: Clásicos Castellanos, 1923.

Musacchio, George. *Milton's Adam and Eve: Fallible Perfection*. New York: Peter Lang, 1991.

Pagels, Elaine. *Adam, Eve, and the Serpent*. New York: Vintage, 1989.

Peale, C. George. "Luís Vélez de Guevara y Dueñas, *La creación del mundo*." *Bulletin of the Comediantes*. 27 (1975): 138-141.

Peers, Allison. "Milton in Spain." *Studies in Philology*. 23 (1926): 169-183.

Pérez Priego, Miguel Angel, ed. *Códice de Autos Viejos*. Madrid: Castalia, 1988.

Phillips, John A. *Eve: The History of an Idea*. San Francisco: Harper & Row, 1984.

Phipps, William E. *Genesis and Gender: Biblical myths of Sexuality and Their Cultural Impact*. New York: Praeger, 1989.

Pierce, Frank. "The 'canto épico' of the Seventeenth and Eighteenth Centuries." *Hispanic Review*. 15 (1947) 1-48.

Praz, Mario. *The Romantic Agony*. Oxford: Oxford UP, 1970.

Preminger, Alex, ed. *Princeton Encyclopedia of Poetry and Poetics*. Princeton: Princeton UP, 1990.

Pritchard, James B. *Ancient Near Eastern Texts Relating to the Old Testament*. Princeton: Princeton UP, 1955.

Reinoso, Félix José. *La inocencia perdida. Poema en dos cantos*. Madrid: Imprenta Real, 1804.

Revard, Stella Purce. *The War in Heaven: 'Paradise Lost' and the Tradition of Satan's Rebellion*. Ithaca: Cornell UP, 1980.

Ricoeur, Paul. *The Symbolism of Evil*. Boston: Beacon, 1967.

Ríos Santos, Antonio Rafael. *Vida y poesía de Félix José Reinoso*. Sevilla: Diputación Provincial de Sevilla, 1989.

Rodríguez-Puértolas, Julio. "La transposición de la realidad en los autos sacramentales de Lope de Vega." *Bulletin Hispanique*, 77 (1970): 96-112.

Rosselló, Víctor. *La caída de Adán*. Barcelona: Heredero de D.P.Riera, 1873.

Rosenberg, David and Harold Bloom. *The Book of J*. New York: Grove Weidenfeld, 1990.

Rosenberg, David. *The Lost Book of Paradise: Adam and Eve in the Garden of Eden*. New York: Hyperion, 1993.

Rouanet, Leo, ed. *Colección de autos, farsas y coloquios del siglo XVI*, Barcelona-Madrid, 1901.

Ruiz Ramón, Francisco. *Historia del teatro español: desde sus orígenes hasta 1900*. Madrid: Cátedra, 1988.

Schurlknight, Donald E. "Alberto Lista: De la supuesta misión de los poetas." *Dieciocho*, 10.2 ( 1987): 168-181.

Shaw, Donald. "La reacción anti-Romántica en España." Ed. David T. Gies. *El romanticismo*. Madrid: Taurus, 1989.

Shawcross, John T. "The Style and Genre of *Paradise Lost*." *New Essays on Paradise Lost*. Ed. Thomas Kranidas. Berkeley: U of California P, 1969.

Smith, Eric. *Some Versions of The Fall: The Myth of the Fall of Man in English Literature*. London: Croom Helm, 1973.

Speiser, E.A. *Genesis*. New York: Doubleday, 1964.

Stone, Merlin. *When God Was A Woman*. New York: Harvest, 1976.

Tarnas, Richard. *The Passion of the Western Mind*. New York: Ballantine, 1991.

Valbuena Prat, Angel. *El sentido católico en la literatura española*. Zaragoza: Partenón, 1940.

Valencia, Juan O. "La visión afectiva-intelectual en una comedia bíblica de Lope: 'La creación del mundo y primera culpa del hombre.'" *Studies in Honor of Everett W. Hesse*. Eds. William C. McCrary and José A. Madrigal. Lincoln: U of Nebraska, 1981.

Vasari, Stephen. "Interpretación temática y simbólica de *El diablo mundo* de Espronceda." Diss. U of California, 1970.

Vega Carpio, Lope de. *La creación del mundo y primera culpa del hombre*. *Obras de Lope de Vega: Autos y coloquios*. Madrid: Biblioteca de Autores Españoles, 1893.

Vélez de Guevara y Dueñas, Luis. *La creación del mundo*. Athens: U of Georgia P, 1974.

Very, Francis George. *The Spanish Corpus Christi Procession: A Literary and Folkloric Study*. Valencia: Tipografía Moderna, 1962.

Wardropper, Bruce. *Introducción al teatro religioso del Siglo de Oro: Evolución del auto sacramental antes de Calderón*. Salamanca: Anaya, 1967.

Welles. M.L. "The Myth of the Golden Age in Gracian's *El Criticón*." *Hispania*, 65.3 (1982): 388-394.

Williams, Arnold. *The Common Expositor: An Account of the Commentaries of Genesis, 1527-1633*. Chapel Hill: U of North Carolina P, 1948.

Williams, N.P. *The Ideas of the Fall and of Original Sin*. London: Longman, Green, 1927.

Woodhull, Marianna. *The epic of 'Paradise Lost'*. New York: G. P. Putnam, 1907.

Ynduráin, Domingo. "Personaje y abstracción." . *El personaje dramático: po-nencias y debates de las VII jornadas de teatro clásico español*. Ed. Lu-ciano García Lorenzo. Madrid: Taurus, 1985.

York, Anthony D. "From Biblical Adam to the American Adam: Evolution of a Literary Type." *University of Dayton Review*, 21.3 (1992): 103-124.

Ziomek, Henry, and Robert White Linker. Introduction. *La creación del mundo*. By Luis Vélez de Guevara y Dueñas. Athens: U of Georgia P, 1974.

# Index

# *Ibérica*

This series of scholarly monographs focuses upon sixteenth- and seventeenth-century Hispanic Theater. *Ibérica* welcomes historical and cultural studies as well as theoretical and critical texts that would enhance our understanding of the *Comedia* as a European phenomenon. Manuscripts may be in English, Spanish or Portuguese, with a minimum of 200 pages. Inquiries and manuscripts should be directed to the general editor:

A. Robert Lauer
Dept. of Modern Languages,
Literature & Linguistics
University of Oklahoma
780 Van Vleet Oval, Room 202
Norman, OK 73019